3 4028 06095 4436
HARRIS COUNTY PUBLIC LIBRARY

Hurricanes: What You Need to Know

363.349 Hur
Hurricanes : what you need
to know

.SM

AUG 0 8 2006

$14.95
ocm63194879

WITHDRAWN

D0870071

WITHDRAWN

HURRICANES
WHAT YOU NEED TO KNOW

GOOSE LANE

Copyright © Goose Lane Editions, 2006.

All rights reserved. No part of this work may be reproduced or used in any form or by any means, electronic or mechanical, including photocopying, recording, or any retrieval system, without the prior written permission of the publisher or a licence from the Canadian Copyright Licensing Agency (Access Copyright). To contact Access Copyright, visit www.accesscopyright.ca or call 1-800-893-5777.

Cover illustration by Corbis.
Cover and interior design by Lisa Rousseau.
Compiled and edited by Rebecca Leaman.
Printed in Canada.
10 9 8 7 6 5 4 3 2 1

Library and Archives Canada Cataloguing in Publication

Hurricanes: what you need to know.

Includes bibliographical references and index.
ISBN 0-86492-453-4

1. Hurricanes. 2. Survival skills.

QC944.H87 2006   363.34'922   C2006-900415-3

Published with the financial support of the Canada Council for the Arts, the Government of Canada through the Book Publishing Industry Development Program, and the New Brunswick Culture and Sports Secretariat.

Goose Lane Editions
500 Beaverbrook Court
Fredericton, New Brunswick
CANADA E3B 5X4
www.gooselane.com

CONTENTS

Checklists

CHAPTER 1

WHAT IS A HURRICANE?

The Anatomy of a Storm

A tropical cyclone is an almost circular storm of extremely low pressure and high winds that spiral inward, accompanied by heavy rainfall. There are three types of tropical cyclones: tropical depressions, tropical storms, and hurricanes, which are the most intense and dangerous.

Hurricanes have three distinctive parts: the eye, the eye wall, and spiral rain bands.

The Eye

One of the most familiar parts of a tropical cyclone is the eye, produced by the intense spiraling of the storm. It is the region where the surface pressure is lowest and the temperature aloft is warmest, and the air in it is slowly sinking. The eye is the innermost zone of the tropical cyclone, but it is not always in the center of the storm. Sometimes it turns or moves in various directions with the storm itself, which continues to move forward on its own course.

The eye is surprisingly calm, with little or no wind. Within it, the skies are often clear, despite the fact that winds and clouds continue to rage around the edge of the eye. As the eye passes over a site, the sky clears and calm prevails. Then, the storm strikes again with high winds from the opposite direction.

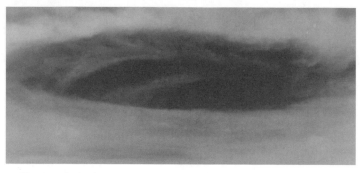

The eye of a hurricane. U.S. Air Force

The Eye Wall

The eye of a tropical cyclone is surrounded by a ring of thunderstorms called the eye wall. The heaviest rain, strongest winds, and worst turbulence are normally in the eye wall. The mechanisms by which the eye and the eye wall are formed are not well understood, but it is generally thought that the feature is a fundamental component of all rotating fluids.

Spiral Rain Bands

Hurricanes are surrounded by bands of heavy convective showers that spiral inward toward the storm's center. Cumulus and cumulonimbus (thunderstorm) clouds rise, and lightning develops in the spiral rain bands at the hurricane's edge.

ALERT Do not relax your precautions if a hurricane suddenly dies down. The eye may be passing directly over you.

The upper eye wall of Hurricane Katrina, captured from a NOAA Hurricane Hunter aircraft over the Gulf of Mexico. The day before making landfall on August 28, 2005, Katrina was a strong Category 4 storm, and the eye was approximately 48 km (30 miles) in diameter. Note the spiral banding in the eye wall clouds and the clear sky above the eye. NOAA

The Life Cycle of a Hurricane

Origin

Many hurricanes that strike North America form in the tropical waters of the Atlantic Ocean or Caribbean Sea, move on a westerly to northerly track, steered by the prevailing wind direction, and strike the mainland on either the Gulf or Atlantic coast.

Hurricanes develop only in certain areas of the earth. Climatologists have defined seven regions of tropical storm formation: the western north Pacific, the eastern north Pacific, the Atlantic, the southwest Indian Ocean, the north Indian Ocean, and two areas off Australia: the southeast Indian Ocean and the southwest Pacific Ocean. The shape of the south Atlantic Ocean basin does not allow storm clouds from Africa enough time over warm water to develop into cyclones, and the waters of the eastern south Pacific are simply too cold for hurricane formation.

In order for tropical cyclones to form, several environmental conditions must be present:

- The cyclone must originate over ocean water that is least 26.5°C (80°F). Hurricanes draw their energy from the warm water of the tropics and the latent heat of condensation.

- The atmosphere must quickly become cooler as the altitude increases. This condition creates instability. If the air is unstable, the warm surface air will continue rising. If winds at all levels of the atmosphere are blowing at the same speed and from the same direction, the disturbance will grow.

- Cyclones form no closer to the equator than approximately 500 kilometres (300 miles). This is because of the Coriolis Force, an effect caused by the turning of the earth, which starts the cyclone spiral and maintains the low pressure of the disturbance. Close to the equator, the Coriolis Force is too weak.

- An upper atmosphere high-pressure area above the growing storm should be present. The air in such high-pressure areas flows outward, pushing away the air that is rising in the storm and drawing even more air up from the low levels.

The Growth of a Hurricane
A hurricane progresses through a series of stages from birth to dissipation. First, it begins as a tropical disturbance: a large area of organized thunderstorms that maintain their identity for more than 24 hours.

If the area of thunderstorms organizes so that a definite rotation develops and winds become strong, the system is upgraded to a tropical depression. At this point, a low-pressure center exists and the storm is given a number.

If winds continue to increase to 63 kilometres per hour (39 miles per hour, or 34 knots), the system becomes a tropical storm and is given a name. The system becomes more organized and the circulation around the center of the storm intensifies.

As surface pressures continue to drop, the storm becomes a hurricane when wind speed reaches 118 kilometres per hour (74 miles per hour, or 64 knots). An eye develops near the center of the storm, with spiral rain bands rotating around it.

FACT

Typhoon Tip (1979), in the northwest Pacific, was the largest tropical cyclone on record. The circulation around it measured 2174 kilometres (about 1350 miles) across.

Storm Track

Tropical cyclones tend to travel common paths, following the predominant wind in the region. For example, late season hurricanes over the Atlantic often begin near Africa, drift west on the trade winds, and then veer northeast as they meet the prevailing winds coming eastward across North America.

The storm track is also affected by the Coriolis Force and by troughs and subtropical ridges in the atmosphere. Predicting the tracks of tropical cyclones would be much easier if the wind currents that drive these storms were fixed in time. The reality is that these currents change constantly, so the tracks of tropical cyclones are difficult to predict.

Power Loss

A hurricane will begin to dissipate when the conditions that enabled it to form and grow no longer exist. When it

Hurricane Size

Hurricanes are typically about 480 kilometres (300 miles) wide, although they vary considerably. Size does not necessarily indicate a hurricane's intensity. At nearly the same location, Floyd (1999, left) was at least twice the size of Andrew (1992, right), although both were Category 4 hurricanes.

Hurricane Floyd
September 14, 1999 @ 1244 UTC

Hurricane Andrew
August 23, 1992 @ 1231 UTC

NOAA

passes over cooler waters or makes landfall, it will begin to dissipate because its main energy source, the warm ocean water, is no longer there. Since land is a rough surface, friction will slow down the movement of the hurricane once it makes landfall, weakening it by disrupting the low-level inflow of warm air.

Tropical Cyclones in Canada
Since Atlantic Canadian waters are much cooler than the tropical waters where hurricanes are formed, hurricanes usually lose their energy source, and most are in the decaying stage of their life cycle by the time they reach these latitudes. Storms that have moved inland also weaken rapidly because they are beyond their source of energy, and

the frictional drag of the land wears them out. The energy of a dissipated storm can continue to move through the atmosphere even when the storm is no longer visible on a weather map. Heavy rain from the very moist tropical air may continue to fall over the region.

Some tropical cyclones undergo post-tropical transition while near Atlantic Canada. As they move into the stronger air streams and cooler air temperatures of the middle latitudes, the storms accelerate, and their rain and wind patterns change. The heaviest rains shift to the left side of the accelerating storm, while the strongest winds occur on the right side. In addition, very high waves can mark the right-hand side of the post-tropical storm's track. Because of these pattern changes, land areas in Canada are frequently affected by the heavy rains but seldom experience the strongest winds.

Saffir-Simpson Scale

Category	Max. sustained wind speed			Min. surface pressure	Storm surge	
	mph	km/h	kt	mb	ft	m
1	74-95	119-153	64-82	980 +	3-5	1.0-1.7
2	96-110	154-177	83-95	979-965	6-8	1.8-2.6
3	111-130	178-209	96-113	964-945	9-12	2.7-3.8
4	131-155	210-249	114-135	944-920	13-18	3.9-5.6
5	156+	250+	136+	919 or less	19+	5.7+

mph = miles per hour
km/h = kilometers per hour
kt = knots

mb = millibars
ft = feet
m = metres

CHAPTER 2

HURRICANE POWER

The Saffir-Simpson Scale

Once a tropical cyclone reaches hurricane strength, it is given a rating from 1 to 5 on the Saffir-Simpson Hurricane Intensity Scale. The Saffir-Simpson Scale gives public safety officials an assessment of the potential wind and storm surge damage from a hurricane. Scale numbers are publicized when a hurricane is within 72 hours of landfall, and they are revised regularly as new observations result in new estimates of the hurricane's disaster potential.

A Category 1 storm has the lowest wind speeds, while a Category 5 hurricane has the highest. These terms are relative, though. Lower category storms can sometimes inflict greater damage than higher category storms, depending on where they strike and the particular hazards they bring. In fact, tropical storms that haven't developed into hurricanes can also produce significant damage and loss of life, mainly due to flooding.

FACT

The destruction caused by Hurricane Camille (1969) provoked a major change in the perception of hurricanes and led to the development of the Saffir-Simpson Hurricane Intensity Scale.

What the Numbers Mean

Category 1 (minimal): Damage primarily to shrubbery, trees, foliage, and unanchored homes. No real damage to other structures. Some damage to poorly constructed signs. Low-lying coastal roads inundated, minor pier damage, some small craft in exposed anchorage torn from moorings.

Category 2 (moderate): Considerable damage to shrubbery and tree foliage; some trees blown down. Major damage to exposed mobile homes. Extensive damage to poorly constructed signs. Some damage to roofing materials of buildings; some window and door damage. No major damage to buildings. Coast roads and low-lying escape routes inland cut by rising water 2 to 4 hours before the arrival of the hurricane's center. Considerable damage to piers. Marinas flooded. Small craft in unprotected anchorage torn from moorings. Evacuation of some shoreline residences and low-lying areas required.

Category 3 (extensive): Foliage torn from trees; large trees blown down. Practically all poorly constructed signs blown down. Some damage to roofing materials of buildings; some window and door damage. Some structural damage to small buildings. Mobile homes destroyed. Serious flooding at coast, with many smaller structures near coast destroyed; larger structures near coast damaged by battering waves and floating debris. Low-lying escape routes inland cut by rising water 3 to 5 hours before hurricane center arrives. Flat terrain of 1.5 metres (5 feet) or less above sea level flooded inland 13 kilometres (8 miles) or more. Evacuation of low-lying residences within several blocks of shoreline possibly required.

Category 4 (extreme): Shrubs and trees blown down; all signs down. Extensive damage to roofing materials, windows and doors. Complete failure of roofs on many small residences. Complete destruction of mobile homes. Flat terrain of 3 metres

A 1x4 board driven through the trunk of a royal palm during Hurricane Andrew (1992). NOAA

(10 feet) or less above sea level flooded inland as far as 9.5 kilometres (6 miles). Major damage to lower floors of structures near shore due to flooding and battering by waves and floating debris. Low-lying escape routes inland cut by rising water 3 to 5 hours before hurricanc center arrives. Major erosion of beaches. Massive evacuation of all residences within 500 metres (500 yards) of shore and of single-story residences within 3 kilometres (2 miles) of shore possibly required.

Category 5 (catastrophic) — Shrubs and trees blown down; considerable damage to roofs of buildings; all signs down. Very severe and extensive damage to windows and doors. Complete failure of roofs on many residences and industrial buildings. Extensive shattering of glass in windows and doors. Some complete building failures. Small buildings overturned or blown away. Complete destruction of mobile homes. Major damage to lower floors of all structures less than 4.5 metres (15 feet) above sea level within 500 metres (500 yards) of shore. Low-lying escape routes inland cut by rising water 3 to 5 hours before hurricane center arrives. Massive evacuation of residential areas on low ground within 16 kilometres (10 miles) of shore possibly required.

FACT

In 1995, Hurricane Luis treated tourists cruising off the coast of Nova Scotia on the *Queen Elizabeth II* to waves of 30 metres (almost 100 feet).

Hurricane Effects

High Winds
Hurricane-force winds can create a hazard for shipping and boating in the form of very high waves on the open ocean. Conditions are even more dangerous near the eye of the

The Galveston Hurricane (1900)

This killer weather system was first detected over the tropical Atlantic on August 27, 1900. The system reached Cuba as a tropical storm on September 3 and moved into the southeastern Gulf of Mexico on September 5, intensifying rapidly as it moved west-northwestward. By the time it reached the Texas coast south of Galveston late on September 8, it was a Category 4 hurricane so destructive that it remains the deadliest weather disaster in United States history. The storm tides that inundated the whole of Galveston Island and nearby parts of the coast were largely responsible for the 8,000-12,000 deaths attributed to the storm, 6,000 in Galveston alone. The damage to property was estimated at $30 million.

After landfall, the Galveston Hurricane continued its destructive path northward through the Great Plains. Losing strength, it turned east-northeastward on September 11, passing across the Great Lakes, southern Ontario and Quebec, New England, the Maritimes, and Newfoundland. Between 52 and 232 deaths in Canada have been attributed to the storm. It was last spotted over the north Atlantic on September 15.

NOAA Coastal Services Center   Galveston 1900

21

hurricane. There, strong winds blowing from all directions generate high waves that seem to move randomly. These unpredictable waves are much more hazardous than those formed by a winter storm, which all move in the same direction.

The strong winds of hurricanes and tropical storms can cause significant damage onshore. When a hurricane approaches a coast or actually makes landfall, the winds can topple trees and destroy houses, buildings, and other structures. In major hurricanes, flying debris becomes a hazard.

FACT

As a rule of thumb, the right side of a hurricane (relative to its direction of travel) is the most dangerous part of the storm. On the left side of the hurricane's track, the counter-clockwise spiraling winds must push back against the forward motion of the storm itself. On the right, however, the hurricane's forward motion reinforces the winds. This is why, in North America, the impact of a hurricane is usually most severe to the north and east of where the eye makes landfall.

Tornadoes

Small tornadoes may develop within hurricanes. In the Northern Hemisphere, they usually develop in the front right quadrant — 12:00 to 3:00 on an imaginary clock face, relative to the overall direction of the hurricane — as it makes landfall and begins to dissipate. The winds at the surface die off quickly, and this creates a strong vertical wind shear that enables tornadoes to develop. In 1969, Hurricane Bertha produced a swarm of over 100 tornadoes on the Texas coast.

Storm Surge

Storm surge is the rapid rise in sea level that occurs as a storm approaches a coastline. The sea level near the coast rises due to

Hurricane Hazel (1954)

Hurricane Hazel struck Toronto on October 15, 1954, killing 81 people and leaving 1,896 families homeless. The record rainfall — up to 225 millimetres (9 inches) in less than 24 hours — could not soak into the ground or escape through storm sewers because the above-average rainfall in the preceding month had already filled the water table. Most of the rain simply ran off the surface into rivers and creeks, rapidly filling them to capacity and beyond. Water coursed through creeks where no creek had ever existed, derailed trains, and washed out roads. Creeks turned into rampaging rivers that tore houses from their foundations, picked up cars and mobile homes, and wrecked boats. Damage was felt throughout southern Ontario and as far away as Ottawa.

A significant outcome of Hurricane Hazel was the formation of the Toronto and Region Conservation Authority (TRCA) and the prioritization of flood control and flood warnings by municipal, provincial, and federal governments. If another storm should duplicate Hazel's path and strength, the city is better prepared, yet risk has not been abolished. Developments remain in the city's floodplains, and, more than fifty years later, residents' memories have faded and a degree of complacency has set in.

Weston Historical Society

23

FACT

The most rainfall ever recorded from a tropical cyclone over 12 hours was 1,144 millimetres (45 inches), dropped by Tropical Cyclone Denise (1966) on Réunion Island, in the Indian Ocean, off the east coast of Africa. In fact, unlucky Réunion has received the five heaviest rainfalls on record.

A beach-front home in Navarre Beach, Florida, damaged by Hurricane Dennis (2005). FEMA / Leif Skoogfors

Hurricane Carol (1954) striking the shore of Old Lyme, Connecticut. Hurricane Carol's huge waves destroyed hundreds of summer cottages and beach front homes in New England. NOAA

the high onshore winds that "pile up" the water near the coast. Also, as a hurricane passes, the extremely low pressure near the center of the storm pulls water upward. The storm surge is the highest on the front right side of Atlantic hurricanes, where onshore winds are the highest. Storm surges can occur even if a hurricane moves along the coast without making landfall. Low-lying areas are the most vulnerable.

Storm surges can have devastating consequences, especially when combined with high tides. The Galveston Hurricane of 1900 killed more people than any other weather disaster in United States history for just that reason.

Heavy Rainfall

Intense rainfall is not directly related to the winds of tropical cyclones but rather to the speed at which the storm is moving and the topography over which it is passing. Slower moving storms produce more rainfall. When a hurricane makes landfall, rainfall can be excessive, particularly if the moist air of the storm is forced over mountain barriers. When a moist pocket of air is forced up into cooler air, the water droplets reach their dew point and rain forms.

Even relatively weak tropical storms can cause extreme rainfall. Because many coastal areas where hurricanes occur are low-lying and fairly flat, the cities can't handle the rapid increase in runoff caused by heavy rains: the water has nowhere to go. Runoff can also be devastating where the land slopes more steeply, bringing flash floods and mud slides like those caused by Hurricane Mitch in 1998.

Inland Flooding

Although most of the devastation associated with tropical storms and hurricanes occurs at sea and along the coast, these storms can cause great damage inland. Flooding along rivers and streams can persist for several days after the storm, but the biggest threat is flash flooding — a rapid rise in water levels due to excessive rainfall. In 1954, the flash floods of the famous Hurricane Hazel killed 81 people in southern Ontario.

Sometimes tropical cyclones produce relatively light rainfall right after landfall and a torrential downpour a few days later, when large quantities of atmospheric moisture are released by a passing disturbance or by the effects of geographic features. This occurred in central Virginia in 1969, when Hurricane Camille hit the mountains and its moist air was lifted into cooler regions. Almost 685 millimetres (27 inches) of rain fell in eight hours, drowning or burying 109 people in flash floods and mud slides.

Factors in Hurricane Damage

The damage caused by tropical cyclones in the Caribbean and Central America, the eastern United States, and eastern Canada varies greatly for several reasons.

- Physical environment: Many small Caribbean islands are easily flooded when a storm passes, and the long flat beaches do not protect areas further inland against a storm surge. In addition, the humid air pushed up over the volcanic mountains of the region can create extra-heavy rainfall.

- Topography: The east coast of the United States is quite varied in topography, but it is also very heavily developed. Even though more hurricanes hit Florida every year than any other state, its islands and coastline remain densely populated. Homes and other structures built directly on beaches and narrow sand spits are especially vulnerable to the storm surges, heavy rains, and high winds of hurricanes.

- Location: Because of high tides, rough topography, and rugged coastline, northern New England and Atlantic Canada are usually not heavily damaged by tropical storms. The warm Gulf Stream, which flows up the coast and veers off into the North Atlantic to the south of the Maritimes and Newfoundland, can act as a preferred path for tropical cyclones, giving them the energy to continue north at high speed. At the same time, it also tends to guide storms away from the coastline. As well, the rugged coastline is quite sparsely populated, with limited coastal development. Thus, although highly destructive storms are infrequent, unpreparedness can lead to catastrophic damage.

- Frequency of storms: Tropical cyclones are much more common in the Caribbean, the Gulf of Mexico, and the southeastern United States than they are farther north, in New England, Ontario, Quebec, and Atlantic Canada. When severe storms hit the same area repeatedly, with limited time for recovery in between, the effects become cumulative.

Building Codes and Construction

If buildings in hurricane-prone areas are designed and constructed to withstand hurricane conditions, hurricanes inflict less damage. Enforcement of existing building codes may be the weakest part of any damage-limitation plan, due to lack of human and financial resources and market pressure to keep building costs as low as possible.

- It is generally agreed that building codes in Central America and the Caribbean could be strengthened, particularly in the case of critical facilities such as emergency shelters and hospitals, which must continue to function during a hurricane rather than simply survive it.

- Building codes in the United States vary because of the diversity of natural disasters that affect different areas of the country. One issue of growing concern, particularly in tourist resort areas, is the heavy development of coastlines and beaches, which are particularly vulnerable to hurricane damage.

- The National Building Code of Canada, mainly concerned with heavy snow loads and high winds, is generally considered adequate for Canada's ordinary experience of extreme weather. Most tropical cyclones that reach Canada cause little structural damage.

Date	Place	Hurricane Name	Number of Deaths
1775	South of Newfoundland		4,000
1780	Barbados, Martinique, St. Eustatius		22,000
1899	Puerto Rico		3,369
1900	Galveston, Texas		8,000 - 12,000
1928	Lake Okeechobee, Puerto Rico, Guadeloupe	Hurricane San Felipe II	3,370
1930	Santo Domingo		8,000
1934	El Salvador, Honduras		3,000
1963	Haiti	Hurricane Flora	8,000
1974	Honduras	Hurricane Fifi	8,000 - 10,000
1998	Honduras, Nicaragua	Hurricane Mitch	10,000

The Great Hurricane of 1780

A hurricane that swept Martinique, St. Eustatius, and Barbados between October 10 and 16, 1780, killed an estimated 22,000 people, and thousands more died offshore. The fatalities of the Great Hurricane of 1780 far exceed those of any other Atlantic hurricane. In fact, the fatalities from this storm exceed the cumulative fatalities in any other year and all other decades.

CHAPTER 3

HURRICANE SEASON

When Is Hurricane Season?

> *June — too soon*
> *July — stand by*
> *August — look out you must*
> *September — remember*
> *October — all over*

This old mariner's verse is rather optimistic: hurricane season for the Atlantic Ocean officially runs from June 1 to November 30 each year. In most years, the first named storm strikes in July, the peak months of the season are August and September, and October can be quite active as well.

El Niño and La Niña Effects

Every three to seven years, there is a change in the way the ocean and the atmosphere interact. El Niño, which is Spanish for "little boy," is the term for a very complex circumstance in which the winds near the equator blow in the direction opposite to their usual path. When the winds change directions, warm water can drift where it doesn't normally go, cold water can appear where warm water is expected, dry areas can get lots of rain, and rainy areas can experience drought.

Worldwide Hurricane Activity

Region	Tropical Storms per year	Hurricanes per year	Months	Peak Months
Western North Pacific	26	16	Year round	August – September
Eastern North Pacific	17	9	May – November	August – September
Atlantic	10	5	May – November	September
Southwest Indian Ocean	10	4	September – May	January – March
Southwest Pacific	9	4	October – May	February
Southeast Indian	7	3	October – May	January – March
North Indian	5	3	April – January	May – November

What does all this have to do with hurricanes? El Niño can create strong winds high in the atmosphere that go in different directions and at different speeds. For hurricanes to form, the winds must be blowing in the same direction and at the same speed from the surface of the sea up to 9,000 metres (30,000 feet) above sea level. Thus El Niño tends to reduce the number of hurricanes that form in the Atlantic.

La Niña, which is Spanish for "little girl," is the opposite of El Niño. Waters that are normally cool get even cooler, waters that are normally warm get even warmer, areas that are normally dry get drier, and areas that are normally wet get wetter. Scientists think that La Niña helps hurricanes form by influencing the wind to blow in the same direction at the same speed. In La Niña years, Atlantic hurricanes are often more plentiful.

Hurricanes vs. Winter Storms

In Atlantic Canada and the northeastern United States, winter storms are much more frequent than tropical or post-tropical cyclones.

Unlike hurricanes, "nor'easters" do not develop in tropical regions. They are caused by intense areas of low pressure that develop off the east coast during late fall, winter, and early spring. As winds blow relatively warm air inland from over the Atlantic Ocean, cold air moves south over the east coast. In the collision of the warm and cold air, rising air cools and condenses into ice crystals or snowflakes. If the air is warm enough, the falling snow melts into rain. Sometimes a layer of warm air above the colder surface produces freezing rain.

These winter storms can be accompanied by hurricane-force winds and heavy precipitation, resulting in storm surges, reduced visibility, and extreme wind chill factors. Nor'easters do most of their damage in coastal areas, in the form of beach erosion and flooding.

FACT

Only three or four tropical cyclones affect Canada every year because most lose their energy over the cold north Atlantic waters. Records show that no Category 3 or higher hurricanes have ever made landfall in Canada.

2005: A Season to Remember

The 2005 Atlantic hurricane season was the most active in recorded history, with 27 named storms, 14 of which

Aftermath of Hurricane Wilma (2005), Key West, Florida. National Weather Service Key West / Jim W. Lee

Hurricane Juan (2003)

For hundreds of storm watchers in Halifax, Nova Scotia, the oceanside Point Pleasant Park seemed the perfect place to be on September 28, 2003. Doug Brown, Senior Park Officer, and Art Sampson, Park Supervisor, knew that the incoming Hurricane Juan was going to be serious. Given their experience with past wind storms and memories of hurricanes Hortense (1996) and Blanche (1975), the two men closed the park gates early. It was an unpopular move, and park patrol staff worked through the evening to evacuate the park and keep people out.

Point Pleasant Park before Hurricane Juan (2003).

The morning after the Category 2 storm struck revealed the extent of the disaster. Boardwalks and grassy areas were buried in beach stones by the storm surge, and some 60,000 to 75,000 trees were flattened as if by one swipe of a giant hand. Hurricane Juan's high winds and storm surge destroyed or heavily damaged 90% of the park's mature forest. The simple precaution of closing the park probably saved dozens of lives.

Hurricane Juan was the most destructive tropical cyclone to hit Atlantic Canada in over a century. Some 100 million trees were lost in Nova Scotia, 1 million of them in Halifax alone. The storm claimed four lives directly and another four in the aftermath. Power outages in Nova Scotia and Prince Edward Island left over 300,000 people without power for up to two weeks.

Point Pleasant Park after Hurricane Juan (2003).
HRM, Point Pleasant Park, Halifax, NS

became hurricanes before the season ended. Of these, seven were major hurricanes — Category 3, 4, or 5 — just one hurricane short of the record set in 1950. Three of the storms reached Category 5. The 2005 season also tied with 1950 for the number of storms formed during October (six), and set a new record for November, with three storms forming in that month.

Names beginning with V and W were used for the first time in 2005. Hurricane Vince formed further to the north and east than any other Atlantic hurricane; it was the first tropical storm to make landfall in mainland Europe. After Hurricane Wilma, the standing list of 21 storm names was exhausted. The World Meteorological Organization (WMO) turned to the Greek alphabet for six more significant storms — Alpha, Beta, Gamma, Delta, Epsilon, and Zeta.

Hurricane Epsilon formed on November 29, just before the official end of the hurricane season, and reached hurricane strength on December 2. When its winds reached speeds of 140 kilometres per hour (85 miles per hour), Epsilon tied Hurricane Nicole (1998) as the second strongest December hurricane on record. Maintaining its force from December 2 to 7, with only a brief drop back to tropical storm status, Hurricane Epsilon is the longest-lasting December hurricane on record. Zeta, the 27th named storm, formed on December 30, after the end of hurricane season. It stayed harmlessly in open water off the central Atlantic coast and weakened to a tropical depression on January 6, 2006.

2005 Records

- 27 named storms (previous record: 21 in 1933)

- 14 hurricanes (previous record: 12 in 1969)

- Four major hurricanes hitting the United States — Dennis, Katrina, Rita, and Wilma (previous record: three, most recently in 2004)

- Three Category 5 hurricanes — Katrina, Rita, and Wilma (previous record: two in 1960 and 1961)

- Seven tropical storms before August 1 (previous record: five in 1997)

- Strongest hurricane in the Atlantic basin — Wilma: 882 mb (previous record: Gilbert, 888 mb, in 1988)

- Three of the six strongest hurricanes on record — Wilma, 882 mb (1st); Rita , 897 mb (4th); Katrina, 902 mb (6th)

- Costliest U.S. hurricane — Katrina, at least $80 billion (previous record: Andrew, $26.5 billion, in 1992 dollars)

- Third-deadliest U.S. Hurricane — Katrina, at least 1,300 deaths (after Galveston, 1900, and San Felipe II, 1928)

The Naming of Storms

Forecasters began naming hurricanes and tropical storms so they could communicate easily with the general public about forecasts, watches, and warnings. More than one hurricane may be raging in the Atlantic at the same time, so naming eliminates confusion about which storm is being described.

For several hundred years, hurricanes in the West Indies were often named after the saint's day on which they occurred. For example, Hurricane San Felipe struck Puerto Rico on September

13, 1876. Another storm struck Puerto Rico on the same day in 1928, and this storm was named Hurricane San Felipe II.

Otherwise, latitude-longitude positions identified storms until George R. Stewart's 1941 novel *Storm* inspired the practice of conferring women's names on them. In 1951, the United States adopted a confusing plan to name storms by a phonetic alphabet (Able, Baker, Charlie), but in 1953 the nation's weather services resumed the simpler custom of using female names.

The practice of using female names exclusively ended in 1978, when names of both genders were used to designate storms in the eastern Pacific. A year later, male and female names were included in lists for the Atlantic and the Gulf of Mexico. Experience has shown that the use of girls' and boys' names in written and spoken communication is shorter, quicker, and causes fewer mistakes than any other hurricane identification system ever used.

Name Lists

Hurricanes are named from six lists, and the name lists rotate, so each is reused every six years. The names on the lists, agreed upon at international meetings of the World Meteorological Organization, have a French, Spanish, Dutch, and English flavor. This is because hurricanes affect numerous countries and are tracked by the general public and the weather services of many nations. Hurricanes are named each year in alphabetical order, but the letters Q, U, X, Y, and Z are not included because of the scarcity of names beginning with those letters.

FACT

In 1979, Hurricane Bob was the first Atlantic hurricane to be given a male name. 1985's Hurricane Bob qualified only briefly as a hurricane, but 1991's Hurricane Bob was responsible for 18 deaths. The name "Bob" was retired after this storm, and "Bill" replaced it in the name list.

The Tropical Prediction Center in Miami, Florida, keeps a constant watch on oceanic storm-breeding grounds. Once a system with counterclockwise circulation and wind speeds of 63 kilometres per hour (39 miles per hour) or greater is identified, the center gives the storm a name from the list for the current year.

Atlantic Storm Names, 2006 - 2011

2006	2007	2008	2009	2010	2011
Alberto	Andrea	Arthur	Ana	Alex	Arlene
Beryl	Barry	Bertha	Bill	Bonnie	Bret
Chris	Chantal	Cristobal	Claudette	Cindy	Colin
Debby	Dean	Dolly	Danny	Danielle	Dennis
Ernesto	Erin	Edouard	Erika	Earl	Emily
Florence	Felix	Fay	Fabian	Fiona	Franklin
Gordon	Gabrielle	Gustav	Grace	Gaston	Gert
Helene	Humberto	Hanna	Henri	Hermine	Harvey
Isaac	Ingrid	Isidore	Isabel	Igor	Irene
Joyce	Jerry	Josephine	Joaquin	Julia	Jose
Kirk	Karen	Kyle	Kate	Karl	Katrina
Leslie	Lorenzo	Lili	Larry	Lisa	Lee
Michael	Melissa	Marco	Mindy	Matthew	Maria
Nadine	Noel	Nana	Nicholas	Nicole	Nate
Oscar	Olga	Omar	Odette	Otto	Ophelia
Patty	Pablo	Paloma	Peter	Paula	Philippe
Rafael	Rebekah	Rene	Rose	Richard	Rita
Sandy	Sebastien	Sally	Sam	Shary	Stan
Tony	Tanya	Teddy	Teresa	Tomas	Tammy
Valerie	Van	Vicky	Victor	Virginie	Vince
William	Wendy	Wilfred	Wanda	Walter	Wilma

Retiring a Name

The only time a list changes is when a storm is so deadly or costly that the future use of its name for a different storm would be insensitive. In that case, at an annual meeting of the WMO committee (called primarily to discuss many other issues), the particular name is stricken from the list and another name is selected to replace it. Retiring the name of a notable storm also prevents confusing a historically well-known storm with a current one. Names that are not retired from the list will be used again in six years.

FACT

Juan (2003) was the first hurricane name to be retired because of a tropical system's impact on Canada.

Retired Atlantic Storm Names

				1954	1955	1956	1957	1958	1959
				Carol Hazel	Connie Diane Ione Janet		Audrey		
1960 Donna	1961 Carla Hattie	1962	1962 Flora	1964 Cleo Dora Hilda	1965 Betsy	1966 Inez	1967 Beulah	1968 Edna	1969 Camille
1970 Celia	1971	1972	1973	1974 Carmen Fifi	1975 Eloise	1976	1977 Anita	1978	1979 David Frederic
1980 Allen	1981	1982	1983 Alicia	1984	1985 Elena Gloria	1986	1987	1988 Gilbert Joan	1989 Hugo
1990 Diana Klaus	1991 Bob	1992 Andrew	1993	1994	1995 Luis Marilyn Opal Roxanne	1996 Caesar Fran Hortense	1997	1998 Georges Mitch	1999 Floyd Lenny
2000 Keith	2001 Allison Iris Michelle	2002 Isabel Lili	2003 Fabian Isabel Juan	2004 Charley Frances Ivan Jeanne					

CHAPTER 4

FORECASTING

International Cooperation

The National Hurricane Center
Through international agreement, the Tropical Prediction Center (TPC) in Miami, Florida, has the responsibility for generating and coordinating tropical cyclone analysis and forecast products for 24 countries in the Americas, including the Caribbean countries, and for the waters of the North Atlantic Ocean, the Caribbean Sea, the Gulf of Mexico, and the eastern North Pacific Ocean.

The National Hurricane Center (NHC) is the branch of the TPC that keeps a continuous watch on developing tropical cyclones during hurricane season, beginning on May 15 in the eastern Pacific and June 1 in the Atlantic and continuing through November 30. The center prepares and issues forecasts, watches, and warnings in text advisories and graphic products.

Although many countries issue their own warnings, they generally base them on direct discussions with, and guidance from, the NHC. During the off-season, the NHC conducts an extensive outreach and education program, training U.S. emergency managers and representatives from many other countries affected by tropical cyclones.

The Canadian Hurricane Centre
In 1985, Hurricane Gloria was forecast to move along the eastern seaboard of North America. Canadians, relying on

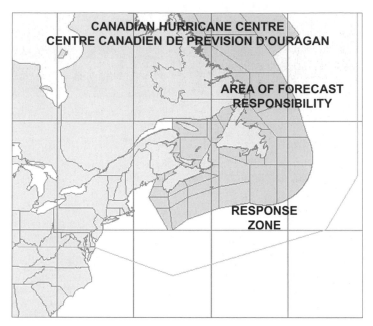

The CHC's response zone and area of forecast responsibility. On average, three or four tropical storms or hurricanes pose a threat to Canada or its territorial waters each year. Reproduced with the permission of Environment Canada, 2005

American sources, were concerned by predictions that this would be the storm of the century. While Gloria did give heavy rain and strong winds to the western part of the Maritime provinces, it was not the intense storm that many had feared. Because of this experience, Environment Canada decided to establish its own Hurricane Centre in metropolitan Halifax, the most populated area in Atlantic Canada.

The Canadian Hurricane Centre (CHC) is part of the Atlantic Storm Prediction Centre, a division of the Meteorological Service of Canada – Atlantic Region. Along with the NHC, the CHC begins to track any tropical cyclone that enters its

Artist's rendering of a NOAA Geostationary Operational Environmental Satellite above the earth. NOAA

response zone. It gathers information on tropical and post-tropical cyclones, predicts their evolution, and assesses their potential impact on its area of forecast responsibility.

Operational meteorologists work around the clock, 365 days a year, to prepare weather forecasts, advisories, and warnings. When a tropical storm or hurricane threatens — when a tropical cyclone, or its effect, is forecast to enter the Canadian Hurricane Centre response zone within 72 hours — the CHC is staffed by its most experienced meteorologists. These individuals have both specialized training from the National Hurricane Center and special expertise in Canadian-style storms.

Storm Tracking Tools

Satellites

Operating the United States' system of environmental satellites is one of the major responsibilities of the National Oceanic and Atmospheric Administration (NOAA). The NOAA National Weather Service (NWS) uses satellite data to create forecasts for television, radio, and weather advisory services. Satellite information is also shared with various federal agencies, with other countries, and with the private sector.

NOAA's operational environmental satellite system is composed of two types of satellites: geostationary operational environmental satellites (GOES) for short-range warning and "now-casting," and polar-orbiting environmental satellites (POES) for longer-term forecasting. Both kinds of satellites are necessary for providing a complete global weather monitoring system.

The CHC and the Atlantic Storm Prediction Centre also gather weather data from two satellites, one polar-orbiting and the other geostationary.

Geostationary Operational Environmental Satellites (GOES)

GOES satellites provide the kind of continuous monitoring necessary for intensive data analysis. They circle the earth

Hurricane Anna (1961), the first hurricane detected by an orbiting satellite,
TIROS III. NOAA

in a geosynchronous orbit, which means they orbit the equatorial plane of the earth at a speed matching the earth's rotation. This allows them to hover continuously over one position on the surface. The geosynchronous plane is about 35,800 kilometres (22,300 miles) above the earth, high enough to allow the satellites a full-disc view of the earth. Because they stay above a fixed spot on the surface, they keep a constant vigil, day and night, for the atmospheric triggers that cause severe weather conditions such as tornadoes, flash floods, hailstorms, and hurricanes. When these conditions develop, the GOES satellites monitor the storms and track their movements.

GOES satellite imagery is used to estimate rainfall during thunderstorms and hurricanes for flash flood warnings, as well as estimate snowfall accumulations and overall extent of snow cover. Such data help meteorologists issue winter storm warnings and spring snow melt advisories. Satellite sensors also detect icefields and map the movements of sea and lake ice.

FACT

Color enhancement of infrared images helps to depict cloud-top temperatures, giving an indication of cloud height: the colder the cloud tops, the higher the clouds extend into the atmosphere.

Polar-Orbiting Environmental Satellites (POES)

Complementing the geostationary satellites are the polar-orbiting satellites. Constantly circling the earth in a sun-synchronous orbit at an altitude of 450 nautical miles (about 840 kilometres / 520 miles), these satellites support large-scale, long-range forecasts and numerous secondary missions. The satellites circle the earth in an almost north-south orbit, passing close to both poles. By operating as a pair, NOAA's polar-orbiting satellites ensure that data for any region of the earth will be no more than six hours old.

The polar orbiters monitor the entire earth, tracking atmospheric variables and providing atmospheric data and cloud images. They provide visible and infrared radiometer data used for imaging purposes, radiation measurements, and temperature profiles. The polar orbiters' ultraviolet sensors also measure ozone levels in the atmosphere and, from mid-September to mid-November, can detect the ozone hole over Antarctica. These satellites send more than 16,000 global measurements daily to the NOAA computers, adding valuable information to forecasting models, especially for remote ocean areas, where conventional data are lacking.

Satellite Images

Satellites take two main types of photographs: infrared and visual. Infrared photographs measure the temperature of the surface below it (earth, sea, clouds, etc.) as it is radiated back into space. Dark and light colors represent the amount of radiation. For example, a white color represents a surface that is a lot colder than a gray color. Visual satellite images provide information about the observed cloud cover as indicated by the amount of solar radiation reflected from the clouds.

Both images can indicate shape and texture. A rough surface would indicate storm-warning cumulus clouds, while a smoother surface would indicate the stratus-type clouds associated with stable atmospheric conditions. The images can determine the temperature of the ocean water, air circulation, and the height of moisture in the atmosphere — factors that are vital in the forecasting of tropical cyclones.

Radar

Weather radar is a valuable tool for determining the location, motion, and intensity of precipitation as it is actually occurring.

Unlike satellite pictures, which show what weather systems look like from above and far away, radar images look upwards from the ground and determine the presence of precipitation through radar echoes. When a hurricane gets close to the coast, it is monitored by land-based weather radars. Doppler weather radars, equipped with the most advanced technology, provide detailed information on changing hurricane wind fields.

Radar works by sending out a radio wave at a very high frequency. When the radio signal hits raindrops, part of

47

Marble Mountain Doppler Radar, Newfoundland & Labrador. Reproduced with the permission of Environment Canada, 2005

the signal bounces back to the radar at the speed of light. The time the signal takes to bounce off of raindrops or snowflakes and return to the station tells how far away the objects are. If the signal does not bounce back, then the area is clear (no rain or snow). The percentage of radar beam that bounces back indicates the amount of rain or snow that is falling. Generally, the higher the percentage of radar beam that bounces back, the more rain or snow. The measured time the signal takes to bounce back to the

Flying into Hurricane Dennis, July, 2005. The Hurricane Hunters of the 53rd Weather Reconnaissance Squadron (U.S. Air Force Reserve) fly into the core of a hurricane to measure wind, pressure, temperature, and humidity and accurately locate the center of the hurricane. U.S. Air Force

station is then translated into a color pixel on a computer-generated image.

Computers
Computers provide meteorologists with simultaneous displays of satellite imagery, numerical guidance, forecast bulletins, and observational data from around the world. Hurricane Forecasting Graphical Interface software, for example, enables CHC forecasters to view historical and real-time tropical cyclone information, plot data, construct storm tracks, and translate the track data into a text bulletin.

To forecast the track and intensity of tropical cyclones, the NHC uses several different mathematical computer models that represent the tropical cyclone and its environment in a greatly simplified manner. Each of the models has particular strengths and weaknesses, and researchers are constantly working to improve them.

It is important to know that these models are run only a few times a day and cannot, therefore, take into account all of the constant short-term changes in the atmosphere. Models cannot produce forecasts more frequently because they require huge amounts of data and long computational times. This is one source of forecast error.

Hurricane forecasters must look at all of the models' results, which frequently give widely different pictures of the future. When the models disagree, hurricane forecasters must use their experience and judgment to decide which model is performing the best under the current conditions.

Buoys
Every hour, data from buoys and marine weather stations is transmitted via satellite to weather centers in North America and elsewhere. Environment Canada's eight Oceanographic Data Acquisition Systems (ODAS) weather buoys, moored off the coasts of Nova Scotia and Newfoundland, carry several types of monitoring equipment. The data received

from weather buoys is particularly useful because it does not require any interpretation — the buoys report actual values. In addition to their use in operational forecasting, warnings, and atmospheric modeling, moored buoy data are used for scientific and research programs, emergency response to chemical spills, legal proceedings, and engineering design.

The National Buoy Data Center of the United States has its own extensive series of moored buoys, and in addition it operates many Coastal-Marine Automated Network (C-MAN) stations on lighthouses, at capes and beaches, on islands near shore, and on offshore platforms. These measure average wind speed and direction, maximum wind speed, wave height and period, atmospheric pressure, air temperature, and sea surface temperature.

FACT

The National Buoy Data Center's Dial-A-Buoy service gives mariners an easy way to obtain up-to-the-hour wind and wave reports from NDBC buoy and C-MAN stations and Environment Canada stations in the Atlantic, Pacific, Gulf of Mexico, and Great Lakes.

Hurricane Hunters

The 53rd Weather Reconnaissance Squadron, located at Keesler Air Force Base in Biloxi, Mississippi, is the only unit in the world flying hurricanes on a routine basis. The "Hurricane Hunters" were activated in 1944 as the 30th Weather Reconnaissance Squadron at Gander, Newfoundland. Their original mission was to fly weather tracks between North America and Allied Western Europe. Since that time, the Hurricane Hunters have had many designations and called many airfields home.

During the hurricane season, the Hurricane Hunters provide surveillance of tropical disturbances and hurricanes in the Atlantic, the Caribbean, and the Gulf of Mexico for the National Hurricane Center in Miami, Florida. They may also fly storms

In June, 2005, NOAA deployed six new weather data buoy stations in the Caribbean, the Gulf of Mexico, and the Atlantic Ocean, and replaced a former station off Pensacola, Florida. NOAA

Buoys at Work

A buoy moored 500 kilometres (300 miles) southeast of Cape Breton measured wind speed and wave height as the eye of Hurricane Danielle (1998) passed nearby.

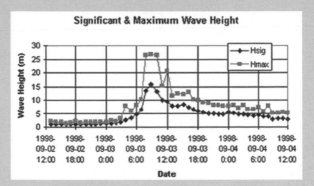

Wave height data, measured by a sensor on the buoy, gathered over 37-minute periods. This graph shows that the waves grew extremely rapidly.

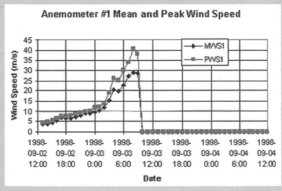

Wind speed measured by one of the two anemometers on the buoy as the hurricane passed. The sudden drop at 10:00 UTC on September 3, during the worst part of the storm, marks the time when the anemometer broke.
Environment Canada

for the Central Pacific Hurricane Center in Honolulu, Hawaii. From November 1 through April 15, the unit flies winter storms off both coasts of the United States in support of the National Center for Environmental Prediction. These missions, flown at high altitude, can be just as challenging as the hurricane missions, with turbulence, lightning, and icing.

Weather Watchers

Both Environment Canada's Meteorological Service of Canada (MSC) and the National Weather Service (NWS) in the United States rely on trained volunteers to provide local observations of severe weather events.

As well as public-spirited citizens with a strong interest in weather, storm spotters often include public safety and law enforcement personnel, citizen band radio operators, and licensed amateur radio operators. Through the CANWARN, ALTAWATCH, and RAQI programs, Canadian amateur radio operators help to create faster and more accurate reports of severe weather events. Similarly, thousands of trained storm spotters in the United States contribute their observations to the NWS-sponsored Skywarn program.

Hurricane Watch Net is an international program involving 35 amateur radio operators in communities from Toronto to Bermuda, throughout the Caribbean, Central America, and Mexico, and across the continental U.S.A. These volunteers provide a continuous path of communications from storm-affected areas to the forecasters in the National Hurricane Center in Miami. Hurricane Watch Net activates whenever a hurricane is within about 480 kilometres (300 miles) of projected landfall or becomes a serious threat to a populated area.

The Voluntary Observing Ship (VOS) Program obtains weather observations from vessels traveling all over the world in the normal course of their business. The program relies on volunteer observers and operates at no monetary cost to the vessel. As an international program under World

Meteorological Organization auspices, the VOS Program lists 63 countries as participants. The United States program is the largest in the world, with approximately 650 vessels actively participating each quarter.

The Saxby Gale of 1869

In 1868, Royal Navy Lieutenant S.M. Saxby realized that on October 5, 1869, the new moon would make its monthly passage closest to earth (perigee) on the equator. He predicted that this combination would cause a severe storm accompanied by a very high tide to strike somewhere on the planet.

Sure enough, on the afternoon of October 4, 1869, in Saint John, New Brunswick, the wind increased to a gale. Rain began falling at six o'clock. By eight-thirty, the wind was blowing at hurricane force. It reached its maximum velocity at about nine, and by ten it began to subside and shifted to the southwest.

The enormous storm surge caused most of the damage. In Moncton, the tide reportedly rose nearly two metres (over six feet) above former records. Numerous people and farm animals drowned in the floods that followed and hundreds of boats were beached due to the high winds. Heavy damage was also reported in Calais, Maine, where 121 boats were reported to be beached. To this day, people tell stories about dramatic rescues from floating haystacks and houses.

CHAPTER 5

STORM WARNING

Communication

As a potential hurricane begins to develop in the Atlantic and move towards North America, the National Hurricane Center and the Canadian Hurricane Centre keep close watch. Advisories are issued every six hours with warning information about where the storm is located, how intense it is, where it is moving, and what precautions should be taken.

National Hurricane Center Bulletins

The National Hurricane Center issues bulletins on tropical weather systems four times a day when a system is active, as well as tropical outlooks and other reports.

Public advisories are issued for all Atlantic tropical or subtropical cyclones, and for eastern Pacific tropical or subtropical cyclones that are threatening land. Public advisories are normally issued every six hours, but they may be issued every two or three hours when coastal watches or warnings are in effect. Special public advisories may be issued at any time due to significant changes in warnings or in the cyclone.

A Hurricane Local Statement (HLS) is issued by a local NWS forecast office when hurricane conditions are being forecast or have been observed. The HLS will contain essential hurricane or tropical storm information in a condensed form, but it will expand on the storm's potential effects on the local area and on any actions declared by local emergency managers.

Canadian Hurricane Centre Bulletins

The CHC issues Prognostic Messages and Information Statements when a tropical storm, hurricane, or post-tropical storm is forecast to enter its response zone within 72 hours. These statements are issued every six hours until the storm no longer poses a threat to Canadian waters or territory. Position and intensity update bulletins are issued every three hours when significant effects from a tropical storm, hurricane, or post-tropical storm are expected over land.

What to Listen For

- Weather **WATCH**: conditions are favorable for the development of severe weather. Watch the sky and listen for updated watches or warnings.

- Weather **ADVISORY**: actual or expected conditions may cause inconvenience or concern but do not pose a serious threat, or conditions may indicate the possibility of severe weather but are not definite enough or too far in the future to justify a warning.

- Weather **WARNING**: hazardous weather is occurring or highly probable. Severe thunderstorm or tornado warnings may be issued less than one hour in advance. Other warnings may be issued six to 12 hours in advance.

Hurricane Watch: Prepare your home and review your plan for evacuation in case a definite warning is issued.

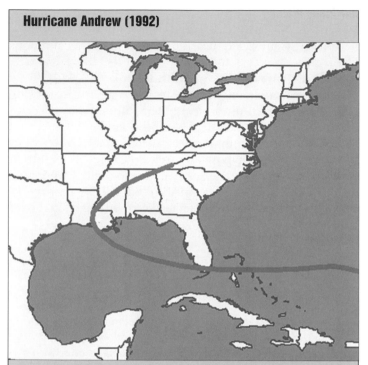

Hurricane Andrew (1992)

Andrew started modestly as a tropical wave that emerged from the west coast of Africa on August 14, 1992. The wave spawned a tropical depression on August 16, which became Tropical Storm Andrew the next day. It blasted its way across south Florida on August 24 as a Category 4 hurricane, continued westward into the Gulf of Mexico, then turned northward to hit the Louisiana coast on August 26 as a Category 3 hurricane. Andrew's peak winds in south Florida destroyed the measuring instruments, so their strength can only be estimated, but an automated station at Fowey Rocks sustained 142 miles per hour (228 kilometres per hour) winds with gusts to 200 miles per hour (272 kilometres per hour) before it stopped reporting. NOAA

Hurricane Watch

A Tropical Storm Watch means that tropical storm conditions could pose a threat to coastal areas, usually within 36 hours. When a hurricane heads for land and is considered a threat to coastal and inland regions, meteorologists issue a hurricane watch for the calculated path. This watch does not mean that a hurricane is definitely going to strike. It means that everyone in the area should watch the weather carefully and be ready to act quickly.

Hurricane Warning: Take precautions immediately, and evacuate at once if local officials tell you to do so.

Hurricane Warning

A Tropical Storm Warning means that tropical storm conditions are expected, usually within 24 hours. A hurricane warning is issued when hurricane-force winds are definitely expected. Coastal areas may receive a hurricane warning when dangerously high water or exceptionally high waves are predicted, even though the anticipated winds may be less than hurricane force. Warnings are seldom issued more than 24 hours in advance. If the hurricane path is unusual or erratic, the warnings may be issued only a few hours before the hurricane strikes. Prepare immediately to ride out the storm safely, and get ready to evacuate.

Pre-recorded weather forecasts are available by telephone throughout Canada and the United States. Check your telephone directory for a local number.

Other Advisories

Land Advisories

- Severe Thunderstorm Watch/Warning: Conditions are favorable for lightning, damaging winds, and hail and/or heavy rainfall. Severe thunderstorms have been sighted or indicated on radar, producing one or more of the following conditions: heavy rain, damaging winds, hail of at least 20 millimetres ($^{3/4}$") in diameter, or intense lightning. Severe thunderstorms may also produce tornadoes.

- Tornado Watch/Warning: Tornadoes may develop. A warning is issued when a tornado has actually been sighted or is indicated by radar. The expected motion, development, and duration will be given in the warning.

- Coastal Flood Watch/Warning: Significant wind-forced flooding is to be expected along low-lying coastal areas if weather patterns develop as forecast.

- Flood Watch/Warning: Flooding is possible or expected within the specified area. A flood watch will include the expected severity (minor, moderate, or major) and where and when the flooding will begin.

- Flood/Flash Flood Warning: A flood/flash flood warning is issued for specific communities, streams, or areas where flooding is imminent or in progress. Take precautions immediately.

- Wind Warning: Expect winds blowing steadily at 60 kilometres per hour (40 miles per hour) or more, or winds gusting to 90 kilometres per hour (58 miles per hour) or more, for at least one hour. Secure or put away loose objects such as outdoor furniture, put your car in the garage, and bring livestock to shelter.

When a flood or flash flood warning is issued, everyone in the area should take precautions immediately.

Marine Wind Warnings

- Small Craft Warning or Advisory: Expect winds of 20 to 33 knots

- Gale Warning: Expect winds of 34 to 47 knots

- Storm Warning: Expect winds of 48 to 63 knots

- Hurricane Force Wind Warning: Expect winds of 64 knots or more

Information Sources

In addition to weather forecasts and advisories aired on commercial and public radio and television stations, up-to-date weather information is available to the public by telephone, on the Internet, and through national Weather Radio services.

Weather Online

Web sites offer comprehensive forecasts and data of many kinds. Web sites are normally available 24 hours a day, seven days a week, free of charge, to anyone who has access to a

Hurricane Ivan (2004) sank and stacked numerous boats at Bayou Grande Marina, Naval Air Station Pensacola, Florida. U.S. Navy

personal computer and the Internet, but remember that major weather events often interrupt access to the Internet.

- Weather.gov: The National Weather Service website. Interactive Weather Information Network (IWIN) provides real-time data and warnings in addition to all standard warnings, watches, advisories, and routine data including geographic forecasts, short term forecasts, zone forecasts, graphical forecasts, select satellite data, and most routine NWS products.

- WeatherOffice.ec.gc.ca: Environment Canada's official online presence for meteorological information and public forecasts, including public advisories, watches, warnings, and the latest radar and satellite imagery. The site is maintained by the Meteorological Service of Canada's national and regional offices and provides all information in both French and English.

Big storms often interrupt Internet access. Be prepared to find information elsewhere in an emergency.

Weather Radio and Public Alert Devices

To benefit from weather alerts broadcast on commercial media, people must be awake, know what time the alert will be transmitted, and tune in to a radio or television station that has chosen to broadcast the alert at just the right time.

Public Alert devices, on the other hand, receive messages about impending life-threatening events on dedicated radio frequencies directly from the responsible government sources in both Canada and the United States — the same official sources that often provide the alert information to the media. The network in the United States is called National Weather Radio (NWR), and in Canada it is called

U.S. Louisiana Army National Guard Staff Sgt. John Jackson checks out portable radios outside the Louisiana Superdome on September 4, 2005, a few nights after Hurricane Katrina struck New Orleans and led to massive flooding. U.S. Army / Master Sgt. Bob Haskell

Weatheradio. These networks are dedicated to delivering alerts without commercials.

Public Alert can be integrated into ordinary electronic equipment that allows the user to play video games, watch a DVD or videotape, listen to the radio, or watch television. Because of their digital data decoding technologies, these alert-capable bedside radios, home security systems, televisions, or phones can receive network broadcasts that automatically trigger alarms 24 hours a day. These alarms take an ever-increasing variety of forms, with many options and functions including adjustable sirens, visual readouts, silent visual modes, chimes, and voice information. Some provide alerts in all U.S. states and territories; others are customized for coverage in Canada; still others operate in both countries.

The primary advantage of owning a Public Alert device is the peace of mind that comes from knowing that all official alert messages will set off an appropriate alarm, even when the household is asleep. There are almost 900 Public Alert transmitters throughout the U.S. states and more than 170 in Canada. Thus an estimated 95% of North Americans are covered by this government-operated public network and can access it simply by acquiring a piece of household electronic equipment that is Public Alert capable.

Storm Summaries

Storm summaries are issued by the Hydrometeorological Prediction Center (HPC) after any named tropical or sub-tropical cyclone has moved inland and public advisories are no longer issued by the National Hurricane Center. In addition, storm summaries are issued for any major winter storms that produce widespread snow or ice. Storm summaries will be transmitted four times a day as long as the threat of severe weather or flash flooding from the storm or its remnants continues.

CHAPTER 6

HURRICANE PREPAREDNESS

There is no way to turn aside the powerful forces of Nature, but modern forecasting techniques give us the advantage of some advance warning.

FACT

Being prepared can make the difference between inconvenience and immense losses.

Taking steps ahead of time can help you cope better if a disaster strikes. Preparing with your family and household and keeping emergency supplies on hand can help you avoid personal injury, assist other people, minimize damage to your property, and survive for at least 72 hours in your home or workplace without help from emergency response officials.

Identify the Risks

Do you live in a potential flood zone, or are high winds the biggest threat? You may find it helpful to prepare a list of the risks you are most likely to face and think about how they might affect your family. While you are preparing for a hurricane, also consider other natural disasters such as earthquakes, technological failures such as power outages, and deliberate acts like terrorism.

Canadians can find out about the most common risks in each region by consulting the Canadian Disaster Database and the Natural Hazards of Canada map, available through Public Safety and Emergency Preparedness Canada (PSEPC).

Information about disaster risks in the United States can be obtained from local American Red Cross chapters, state and local emergency measures offices, the Federal Emergency Management Agency (FEMA), or on the Internet at Hazardmaps.gov.

Family Emergency Plan

Having a plan that outlines where you will go and how you will keep in touch with members of your family if a severe storm hits will decrease mental anguish and can save lives.

By definition emergencies happen unexpectedly, often too suddenly to allow you to choose a shelter or pack up supplies, so prepare a list of what to do at home, school or work if a disaster strikes. (See the checklists on pages 134-137.) Divide up tasks so that every member of your household participates as much as possible. Write down the details and make sure everybody has a copy of the plan.

Make sure that your Family Emergency Plan takes into account the special requirements of any family members who may have limited physical mobility, memory problems, or other health concerns.

- Know the safe places in your home. Decide where to take shelter during different situations such as hurricanes or earthquakes. Practice taking cover in the safe places at least once a year. Repeating this kind of safety drill — practicing exactly where to go and what to do — is important for everyone but especially essential for children, so they know what to expect and don't forget the instructions over time.

- Agree on an alternate meeting place and shelter. Make sure each family member knows what to do at home, at school, or at work if family members become separated or if it is impossible to get home. Decide where you will meet if you are separated during a disaster, and choose a place, such as a friend's house or a hotel, where you can stay for a few days in case you are evacuated. When choosing your shelter, remember that bridges may be out and roads may be blocked.

- Plan for your pets. They may not be permitted in emergency shelters, so find a pet-friendly hotel or friend's home in advance.

- Select an out-of-the-area contact. Pick someone each member of the family can call or e-mail in case of an emergency, and include that person in your planning. Be sure to choose someone who lives far enough away not to be affected by the same situation. This person, ideally a relative or close family friend, should agree to pass news on to other family members if you get separated and contact him or her from different places. Each member of the household should memorize this person's phone number and address and keep the information handy at all times.

- If you live alone, develop an emergency plan for yourself with links to friends and neighbors.

TIP

If someone in your care relies on electrically powered life-sustaining equipment, register with your electric supply authority and your community emergency program.

Other Emergency Plans

Schools and Day-Care

Learn about the emergency plans of your children's schools or day-care center. For example, you will need to know whether your children will be kept at school until you or a designated adult can pick them up, or if they will be sent home on their own. Be sure that the school has up-to-date contact information for you. Find out ahead of time what type of authorization the school requires to release a child to someone else should you not be able to pick up your child yourself. Keep in mind that school telephones may be overwhelmed with calls during an emergency. To help your children, you and they need to know both school plans and family plans ahead of time.

Ask the same questions at sports and recreation facilities, youth centers, shopping malls — wherever your children are most likely to be when they are not at home with you. Talk about emergency planning with the parents of your children's friends as well.

In the Workplace

Your place of employment may have an emergency plan. Ask questions: what would be your role in case of a disaster? What are the evacuation procedures? What are the escape

TIP

Make sure schools have comprehensive, up-to-date contact information for all adults sharing responsibility for your children.

routes from each work station? Is there an alternate work site in case of emergency? Always make sure that corridors and aisles leading to emergency exits are clear of obstruction.

On the Road

Travel with a battery-powered radio, flashlight, and extra batteries. In a hotel, keep your clothing and footwear near the bed in case you have to leave in a hurry during the night. Keep important papers together and easy to pick up. As soon as you arrive, identify the safest place in your hotel room to take shelter (such as under a table). Know where the stairways are; read any information in the room about evacuation procedures; and be prepared to follow instructions.

Prepare Your Home

- Go through your home with other household members and imagine what could happen to each part of it during a hurricane, a violent earthquake, or other disaster that might strike your area. Identify ways to make your home and property more secure, and plan what you will do in various situations.

- Keep important numbers – including fire, police, and ambulance – near your telephone, and program them into cordless telephones and cellphones.

- Teach everybody in the household how to turn off the water, electricity, and gas. Clearly label the on-off positions for these utilities. If your home is equipped with natural gas, tie or tape the appropriate wrench to the pipe to turn off the gas.

- Keep one household fire extinguisher handy near the kitchen and others elsewhere in the house, and teach every member of your family how to use them. Test and recharge your fire extinguishers periodically according to the manufacturer's instructions.

- Discuss insurance coverage with your broker. Make sure that you have the right kind of insurance for the range of risks that may occur in your area.

- Make an inventory of the valuable things you own and store a video or photographs of them for insurance purposes.

Prepare Yourself

First Aid

Learning some basic first aid is a preparedness measure that will prove useful and may mean the difference between life and death. First aid training will help you to help yourself and those around you, perhaps including professional emergency aid workers, and it will enable you to help injured people evacuate a building or a dangerous area. In an emergency, remember that you should always tend to your own well-being first so you remain strong enough to help others.

Keeping Your Affairs in Order

- Bank machines and credit card systems may not work in an emergency, so it may be wise to keep some extra cash on hand in hurricane season.

- Collect important documents in a sturdy waterproof container: birth certificates, identification, credit cards, insurance documents, health records, prescriptions, etc. If you need to evacuate at short notice, they will be ready to travel with you.

- If you keep important records on a computer, make back-up copies on a disk or other portable device and store them with your other documents.

- Copies of essential documents should also be kept in a safe place outside your home, such as a safety deposit box or the home of a relative who lives out of town.

Prepare Your Pets and Livestock

- Make sure that all animals — pets or livestock — have tattoos or electronic implants or are wearing identification tags or leg bands, in case they become lost. Take photographs to keep with your important papers.

- Do not leave your pets behind if you leave home. Make a list of hotels that will accept pets, or make arrangements with friends outside your storm-warning area.

- Animals may be at risk of disease if they have to be boarded with other animals who may not be vaccinated, if they are injured, or if they come into contact with contaminated water. All standard vaccinations should be kept up to date and the certificates stored with other important documents.

A wandering dog in the devastated Lower 9th Ward of New Orleans, Louisiana, following Hurricane Katrina (2005). FEMA / Andrea Booher

- Evacuation of livestock requires extensive planning. Farmers may need to consider how an evacuation will impact them financially, which animals to sell, what resources are needed to evacuate the animals, and where evacuated animals could be taken. If evacuation from a storm area is not possible, livestock are generally safest in a large field that is free of trees or debris that could be moved by the wind.

Emergency Kits

You could be anywhere when a disaster strikes, but it is likely that you will be at home, at work, or in your car. Put together a home or evacuation emergency kit of supplies that can help you survive the emergency and, if necessary, make you self-sufficient for three days or longer.

Emergency kits should be portable, so put supplies in an easy-to-carry container such as a duffel bag or small plastic bin, ready to take with you. Store the kit in an easily accessible place, such as a closet shelf on the main floor. If you live in an area where hurricanes are a frequent threat, you might prepare a personalized kit in a backpack for each member of the family, ready to go in case you need to evacuate.

Contents of an Emergency Kit

For everyone:

- Food that won't spoil, such as canned or dry foods

- First aid kit

- Money and essential papers

- Extra set of car keys

- Battery-powered Weather Radio/Public Alert device and portable radio

- Food, water, crate or kennel, and other requirements for pets

For each person:

- Water: 4 litres (one gallon) per day

- Prescription medicines

- One change of clothing and shoes

- One blanket or sleeping bag

- One flashlight, with extra batteries

- Special items for infant, elderly, or disabled family members

Store these emergency supplies in backpacks, duffel bags, or plastic bins to carry with you if you need to evacuate, and store important documents that you do not wish to leave in the emergency kit in a waterproof container that you can pick up quickly to take with you.

Keep a smaller emergency kit in the trunk of your car and another in your workplace. You might keep some additional supplies in a tool shed or garage in case you have to leave your home and can't go back inside.

Practice Your Plan

An emergency can happen anytime, anywhere. Practice often helps people feel less disoriented and better organized in case of a disaster, even in the middle of the night or in the winter. A practice drill at the beginning of each hurricane season will help everyone to remember exactly what to do in a real emergency. It will also help you to spot any parts of your plan that may need to be changed.

Emergency Drills

- Remind each member of the family where and how to turn off the water, gas and electricity supply to your home. Prepare large, easy-to-see signs for water and gas shut-offs and the main circuit breaker.

- Be sure that every member of your family knows the agreed-upon meeting places, phone numbers and safety rules.

- Remind each person of where to find a fire extinguisher and how to use it.

- Put yourselves physically in each room of your home and practice evacuation

TIP

Remember to practice taking along your emergency kit.

When Hurricane Season Begins . . .

- Verify the telephone numbers and personal information of everyone on the plan.

- Print updated copies of the emergency plan for all the members of your family, your children's school, and other frequently-used facilities.

- Change the batteries in your flashlights and portable radio, and replace the spare batteries.

- Replenish your emergency kits. Replace the bottled water, ensure that all food is still safe to eat, and check that medicines have not expired.

Your Community

Learn about your community's emergency plans and authorities. Who is in charge? Whom should you call? What might you be asked to do in an emergency? Find out where emergency shelters are located and whether there are designated emergency routes to them or out of town.

TIP

The National Weather Service sponsors Hurricane Awareness Week before each hurricane season. For dates and activities, listen to NOAA Weather Radio and check NWS Web sites and local media.

Identify the closest emergency services offices, including fire, police, ambulance, and public works, such as gas and electrical utilities. Record their telephone numbers, which you can probably find near the front of your phone book, in a list near the telephone.

Is Your Community Prepared?

To help Americans prepare for the ravages of extreme weather, the National Weather Service has designed StormReady, a program aimed at arming America's communities with the communication and safety skills necessary to save lives and property. More information is available on the Internet at www.nws.noaa.gov/stormready.

In Canada, Safeguard is the national information program. Based on partnerships, it aims to increase public awareness of emergency preparedness. The Safeguard program brings together government, private organizations, and voluntary agencies involved in emergency preparedness, response, recovery, and mitigation of effects. More information is available at www.safeguard.ca.

High-Rise Buildings

If you live in an apartment building or work in a high-rise, that building should have its own emergency plan. If you are unaware of such a plan, take steps to find out about it, or else, with the help of trained emergency personnel, join with your fellow residents to draw up a plan. Be sure you understand the various levels of alarm in your building and the proper response to each. Know what to do in the event of an alarm and the building's evacuation plan. Know the

An apartment building wall peeled off by Hurricane Andrew (1992). NOAA

location of each exit stairwell on your floor, and identify them as primary (closest) and secondary exits.

Never use the elevator to evacuate during an alarm. A power outage will turn the elevator into a trap.

Mobile Homes

Owners and residents of mobile homes must take special care to protect themselves and their property. Site the trailer in consideration of the direction from which storms usually come. Face the narrow end in that direction to make a smaller target, and try to position the trailer near a natural windbreak such as a hill or clump of trees. Make sure your mobile home is anchored securely. Consult the

A mobile home in Barco, North Carolina, destroyed by the roots of a tree blown over by Hurricane Bonnie (1998). FEMA / Dave Gatley

manufacturer for information on effective tie-down systems. When a severe storm approaches, you should seek shelter in a more secure building.

ALERT

If you live in a mobile home, evacuate to a safer location when you hear a hurricane warning. Do not wait for a general evacuation order.

Neighborhoods, Apartment Buildings, and Mobile Home Parks

A community working together during an emergency can increase everyone's safety and help minimize everyone's risk.

- Talk to your neighbors about how you can work together during an emergency.

- Find out who has specialized equipment, such as a generator, ladders, or a small boat.

- Find out who has special expertise, such as medical knowledge, trade skills, or administrative ability.

- Decide who will check on elderly or disabled neighbors.

- Make back-up plans for children in case their parents can't get home to care for them.

- Share individual plans and communicate when you put them into effect so your neighbors know you're safe.

CHAPTER 7

BATTEN DOWN THE HATCHES

Strengthening Your Home

During a hurricane, homes may be damaged or destroyed by high winds and waves. Debris can break windows and doors, allowing high winds inside the home. In extreme storms, the force of the wind alone can cause weak places in your home to fail.

After Hurricane Andrew (1992), a team of experts examined homes that had failed and ones that had survived. They found four areas that should be checked for weakness: the roof, the windows, the doors, and, if you have one, the garage door.

Outdoors

It's easy to take care of the outside of your home before hurricane season but impossible to catch up on these tasks once a hurricane warning has been issued.

- Trim off dead or weak tree branches and cut down dead trees to keep them from falling on or being driven into your house.

- Clear debris from rain gutters and downspouts in preparation for heavy rainfall.

- Consider checking the drainage around the house to reduce the possibility of basement flooding.

- If you live in a flood-prone area, rcmove all chemical products from the basement and move all irreplaceable belongings to an upper floor.

Roof

During a windstorm, the force of the wind pushes against the outside of your home. That force is transferred from your roof to the exterior walls and finally to the foundation. Homes can be damaged or destroyed when the energy from the wind is not properly transferred to the ground.

The connection between the roof and the walls must be strong enough to resist the "uplift" effect of strong winds. Roof trusses or rafters should be tied properly to exterior walls with metal hurricane connectors or straps.

Homes with gabled roofs are more likely to suffer damage during a hurricane than those with hip or flat roofs. The A-shaped end wall of a home with a gabled roof takes a beating during a hurricane, and those that are not properly braced can collapse, causing major damage to the roof.

In most homes, gabled roofs are built using manufactured trusses. Sheets of roof sheathing, often plywood, are fastened to the trusses with nails or staples, and roofing material is fastened to the sheathing. In many cases, the only thing holding the trusses in place is the plywood on top. This may not be enough to hold the roof in place during a hurricane.

Notice how the plywood is attached to the truss system in your house. If most of the large nails or staples coming through the sheathing have missed the trusses, consider having the sheathing properly installed. Installing additional truss bracing makes your roof's truss system much stronger.

A construction worker attaches hurricane straps to a new home in Deerfield Beach, Florida, 1999. FEMA / G. Mathieson

Exterior Doors and Windows

The exterior walls, doors, and windows are the protective shell of your home. If this protective shell is broken, high winds can enter and put pressure on the interior of your roof and walls, causing damage. You can protect your home by strengthening the doors and windows.

- Double-entry doors: In a double-entry door system, one door is active and one is inactive. Check to see how the fixed half is secured at the top and bottom. The bolts or pins that secure most doors are not strong enough to withstand hurricane winds, so check with your local building supply store to find out what kind of bolt system will work for your door.

- Double-wide garage doors: Two-car garage doors are so large that they wobble when attacked by high winds. Wind pressure can pull them out of their tracks or collapse them. If garage doors fail, high winds can enter your home through the garage and blow out doors, windows, walls, and even the roof.

  - Check the track on your garage door. With both hands, grab a section of each track and see if it is loose or if it can be twisted. If so, a stronger track should be installed.

  - Your garage door may need heavier hinges and stronger supports. Many doors can be reinforced at their weakest points by installing horizontal bracing onto each panel. Ask your local building supplier if a retrofit kit is available for your particular door.

These shutters on a house in New Bern, North Carolina, provide good protection against hurricane-force winds. Permanently mounted hinges make them easy to put up and take down. FEMA / Dave Saville

- Windows: Tape does not prevent windows from breaking. Installing storm shutters over all exposed windows and other glass surfaces is one of the easiest and most effective ways to protect your home. You should cover all windows, French doors, sliding glass doors, and skylights. Before installing shutters, check with your municipal government to find out if you need a building permit.

TIP

Get your shutters ready before hurricane season. Mark each according to which window it fits, and store them so you can install them easily during a hurricane watch.

- For information on the many types of manufactured shutters, check with your local building
  supply store. When installing, follow the
  manufacturer's instructions carefully.

- Homemade shutters made of $5/8"$marine
  plywood can be installed on all types of
  homes. If installed properly, they can offer a
  high level of protection from flying debris.

Special Precautions for Mobile Homes

Mobile homes are particularly vulnerable to hurricane-
force winds. Anchor your mobile home with over-the-top
or frame ties. When a storm threatens, secure your home
as best you can, then take refuge with friends or relatives
or at a public shelter. Before you leave, take the following
precautions:

- Pack breakables in boxes and put them on the
  floor.

- Remove mirrors and tape them. Wrap mirrors and
  lamps in blankets and place them in the bathtub
  or shower.

- Install hurricane shutters or precut $5/8"$ marine
  plywood on all windows.

- Shut off utilities and disconnect electricity, sewer,
  and water lines. Shut off propane tanks, and leave
  them outside, securely anchored.

- Store awnings, folding furniture, trash cans, and
  other loose outdoor objects.

Protect Against Flood Damage

Property owners in vulnerable areas should take measures to limit possible damage from storm surges or flash floods. Elevating your entire home is the most effective, but there are also other, relatively inexpensive ways to protect your home and property against flooding.

- Relocate the electrical box, the water heater and the heating system to an upper floor. If this is impossible, raise them at least 30 centimetres (12 inches) above the usual flood level in your area. Your municipal building officials can identify this safe level for you.

- Anchor the fuel tank to the floor or wall to prevent it from overturning, spilling its contents, and floating. Metal structural supports and fasteners must be noncorrosive, and wooden structural supports must be pressure treated.

Houses on the beach are particularly at risk from storm surge during a hurricane. FEMA

Hurricane Watch

Severe weather can develop very quickly, so listen regularly to weather forecasts on local media outlets or Weather Radio during hurricane season. When a storm threatens, stay tuned to public weather advisories, keep track of its progress, and be prepared to carry out your Family Emergency Plan. If you're working or playing outside, be aware of changing weather conditions and be ready to act quickly.

Take Care of Yourself, Your Family, and Your Animals

When a hurricane watch or warning is issued:

- Secure or bring inside any items that might be blown away or torn loose. Garbage cans, gardening tools, toys, porch furniture, and other objects become weapons of destruction when they are picked up by the wind and hurled against buildings or vehicles. Remove outdoor antennas, if possible.

- Fuel up the family vehicle and review your evacuation routes.

- Move small children, other vulnerable family members, and pets and livestock to a pre-determined safe location.

- Secure all boats and items left loose on piers in boathouses.

- Leave any low-lying beach or other area that may be swept by high tides or storm waves. Remember, the roads to safer areas may become flooded before the main portion of the storm arrives.

- If your home is strongly built and out of danger, plan to stay there during the hurricane. Gather your emergency kit and keep it close at hand. Turn the refrigerator and freezer to their coldest settings. Store drinking water in clean bathtubs, jugs, bottles, and cooking utensils. Board up the windows or protect them with storm shutters.

- Make your preparations quickly, then take cover, and stay there until the weather has calmed and the danger has passed.

ALERT

If your home is sturdy, well protected, and away from flood danger, go indoors and stay there, away from windows, doors, and fireplaces, until the storm is over, unless public officials tell you to evacuate.

Take Care of Your Business

If a hurricane threatens the area where your business is located, take action before the storm strikes to minimize damage and lost productivity.

- Clear out areas with extensive glass frontage as much as possible. If you have shutters, use them. Otherwise, use precut 5/8" marine plywood to board up doors and windows.

- Remove outdoor hanging signs.

- Bring inside or secure any objects that might become airborne in strong winds and cause damage.

- Secure showcases. Use plywood to protect glass showcases, or, if possible, turn the glass side toward an inside wall.

- Move merchandise that cannot be stored away from any glass and cover it with tarpaulins or heavy plastic.

If flooding is likely:

- Store as much merchandise as you can as high as possible off the floor, especially goods that could be in short supply after the storm.

- Secure all goods in warehouses off the floor, and place sandbags in spaces where water could enter.

- Remove papers from lower drawers of desks and file cabinets and place them in plastic bags or containers on top of the cabinets.

- Turn off water heaters, stoves, pilot lights, and other burners.

ALERT

Plan to leave when a hurricane watch has been issued if you . . .

- **Live in a mobile home. It is unsafe in high winds no matter how well it is fastened to the ground.**

- **Live on the coastline or an offshore island or near a river or a flood plain.**

- **Live in a high-rise building. Hurricane winds are stronger at higher elevations.**

The frame of a mobile home remains anchored by its tie-downs after the passage of Hurricane Andrew (1992), but the rest of the home is gone.
NOAA

A sign west of Englehard, North Carolina, marks the evacuation route for people escaping Hurricane Isabel (2003). FEMA / Cynthia Hunter

CHAPTER 8

DURING THE STORM

Hurricanes

If a hurricane warning has been issued and you live on the coast or in a low-lying area near the coast, you should move inland and to higher ground. The high winds create huge waves at sea which, when they reach the shore, may become tidal waves or storm surges.

No matter how strongly you are tempted to go down to the water to watch the storm, do not do it. Do not even think about surfing. The waves are thrilling, but they are deadly. Most people who are killed during hurricanes are caught in large waves, storm surges, or floods.

As a rule, hurricanes move slowly and batter communities for several hours. If the eye of the hurricane passes over, there will be a lull in the wind lasting from two or three minutes to half an hour. Stay indoors, away from windows, doors, and fireplaces.

Keep in touch frequently with family members, if you are not all in the same location. You can use a cellular telephone during a severe storm, but it is not always safe to use a land-line telephone when there is lightning.

Make emergency repairs only, and remember that once the eye has passed over, the winds will return from the opposite direction with possibly even greater force. Monitor the storm's progress and listen for warnings or instructions from local officials.

If you are advised by officials to evacuate, do so at once. Take your emergency kit with you.

 Do not go down to the water to watch the storm or to surf. The waves are killers.

High-Rise Safety

In an apartment building, office tower, hotel, or other high-rise, always take the precaution of knowing where the closest emergency exit stairway is, and make sure you know another way out in case your first choice is blocked. If a hurricane strikes while you're in a high-rise, determine which is less hazardous: staying put or evacuating.

If you leave:

- Listen for and follow instructions.

- Take your emergency kit.

- Do not use elevators.

- Stay to the right while going down stairs to allow emergency workers to come up.

If you can't leave:

- Listen for and follow instructions.

- Move away from exterior walls.

- Move away from file cabinets, bookshelves, or other things that might fall.

- Face away from windows and glass.

- Take cover behind or under a desk or table if things are falling.

Tornadoes

Tornadoes may develop around hurricanes in coastal regions. Inland, they develop as deadly storms in their own right. They can move very fast, sometimes too fast for public warnings to be fully effective. When you see or hear a tornado coming, protect yourself immediately.

Tornado Warning Signs

- Severe thunderstorms, with frequent thunder and lightning

- An extremely dark sky, sometimes highlighted by green or yellow clouds

- A rumbling sound, like a freight train, or a whistling sound, like a jet plane

- A funnel cloud at the rear base of a thundercloud, often behind a curtain of heavy rain or hail

A tornado heading straight for you may appear to be standing still.

Indoors

Stay away from windows, doors, and outside walls. The safest place is in the basement. If there is no basement, take cover under a stairway, or stay in a small interior ground floor room such as a bathroom, closet, or hallway. Failing that, protect yourself by taking shelter under a heavy table or desk. In all cases, stay away from windows, outside walls, and doors. Go to the center of the house or the side away from the storm.

- In an office or apartment building, take shelter in an inner hallway or room, ideally in the basement or on the ground floor. Do not use the elevator, and stay away from windows.

- Avoid or leave buildings with large, unsupported roofs, such as arenas, supermarkets, and barns. Wide-span roofs may collapse if a tornado hits them. If you are caught in such a building, get under the lowest roof section, go to an inside hallway or small room, or get under something sturdy.

- Avoid mobile homes. More than 50% of all deaths from tornadoes happen in mobile homes. Take shelter elsewhere, preferably in a building with a strong foundation. If no shelter is available, lie down in a ditch away from the mobile home. However, beware of flooding from downpours and be prepared to move.

Outdoors

- If you are driving and spot a tornado in the distance, try to get to a nearby shelter. If the tornado is close, get out of your car and take cover in a low-lying area such as a ditch, but stay alert for flooding. Do not remain in your car. You may be trapped if the twisting wind overturns it.

- If a tornado catches you in the open, move away from its path at a right angle. If you are unable to avoid it, find a ditch, ravine, or other depression and lie flat. If no shelter can be found, hang onto a small tree or shrub that can anchor you but not fall on you.

- In all cases, get as close to the ground as possible, protect your head, and watch for flying debris. Small objects such as sticks and straws can become lethal weapons when driven by a tornado.

Flooding

Between 1970 and 1999, more people died from freshwater flooding associated with tropical cyclones than from any other hurricane-related hazard.

- When there is immediate danger of flooding, shut off the electricity. If the area around the fuse box or circuit breaker is wet, stand on a dry board and shut off the power with a dry wooden stick.

- Turn off basement furnaces and outside gas valves.

- Disconnect eavestroughs if they are connected to the house sewer, and plug basement sewer drains and toilet connections with a wooden stopper.

- Try to move furniture, electrical appliances, and other belongings to floors above ground level. Remove toxic substances such as pesticides and insecticides from the flood area to prevent immediate pollution of your own surroundings as well as eventual environmental pollution.

- In some cases, homes may be protected with sandbags or polyethylene barriers. This approach

Wading through the flood caused by Hurricane Katrina (2005) in New Orleans. FEMA / Marty Bahamonde

requires specific instructions from your local emergency officials.

- You may be asked to evacuate. Keep your radio on to find out what areas are affected, as well as what roads are safe, where to go, and what to do if the local emergency team asks you to leave your home.

- Use great caution when crossing a flooded area on foot. Fast water could sweep you away and drown you, regardless of your ability to swim. Swiftly moving shallow water can be deadly, too.

- Try not to cross a flooded area in a car. Water over roads and in underpasses may be deeper than it looks. You could get stuck, or your car might stall, break down, or even be swept away.

- You may want to avoid crossing bridges if the water is high and flowing quickly.

If you are caught in fast-rising water and your car stalls, abandon it and save yourself and your passengers.

Downed Power Lines

If you see a downed power line, call your electric supply authority to report its exact location. Keep back a minimum of 10 metres (33 feet) from wires or anything in contact with them, and warn others of the danger.

Always assume that any downed line is live. It is difficult to distinguish between power lines and telephone, cable, or other utility lines, and such lines also carry sufficient power to hurt you. Treat all lines as a danger.

Power Outages

- Turn off all tools, appliances, and electronic equipment, and turn home heating thermostats down to minimum. If they start up automatically when service is restored, they may cause injury, damage, or fire, and they will contribute to over-loading the newly restored system.

- If you must use a candle, fix it firmly it in a heatproof candleholder placed on a stable surface. Never leave lit candles unattended.

- If your house is protected from groundwater by a sump pump, it won't work if the power fails. Clear any valuable objects from the basement floor in case of flooding.

- Before considering the use of an emergency home generator during a power failure, check with furnace, appliance, and lighting fixture dealers or manufacturers regarding power requirements and proper operating procedures.

TIP

If someone in the home relies on electrically powered life-sustaining equipment, register with your electric supply authority and your community emergency program.

Food Safety

Monitor food stored in refrigerators and freezers for signs of spoilage after a power outage of more than two hours. The refrigerator will lose its effectiveness sooner than the freezer. To keep milk, other dairy products, meat, fish, eggs, gravy, and spoilable leftovers edible for a little longer, pack them into a cooler, surrounded by ice. Inexpensive Styrofoam coolers are fine for this purpose. Use a digital quick-response thermometer to check the temperature of your food right before you cook or eat it. Throw away any food with a temperature higher than 4°C (40°F).

If the door of a half-full freezer has been kept closed, food should stay frozen for 24 hours. A full freezer will hold food safely for 48 hours. Food that has begun to defrost should be cooked immediately or destroyed in accordance with instructions from your local public health authorities.

As a general precaution, keep a bag of ice cubes in the freezer. If you return home after a period of absence and find that the ice has melted and refrozen, there is a good chance that the food is spoiled.

ALERT

If the power is out for less than two hours, food in your refrigerator and freezer will be safe. If it's out longer than two hours, take precautions.

Safe Drinking Water

When the power goes out, water purification systems may not function fully. At first, you can obtain some safe water from your hot water tank and from toilet tanks (not toilet bowls). Otherwise, safe water for drinking, cooking, and personal hygiene includes bottled, boiled, or treated water. Your local health department can make specific recommendations for boiling or treating water in your area. In general:

- Do not use contaminated water to wash dishes, brush your teeth, wash and prepare food, wash your hands, make ice, or make baby formula. If possible, use baby formula that does not need to have water added. You can use an alcohol-based hand sanitizer to wash your hands.

- If you use bottled water, be sure it came from a safe source. If you do not know that the water came from a safe source, you should boil or treat it before you use it. Use only bottled, boiled, or treated water until your supply is tested and found safe.

- Boiling water is the preferred way to kill harmful bacteria and parasites. Bringing water to a rolling boil for one minute will kill most organisms. To improve the flat taste, aerate it by pouring it back and forth between two containers, allow it to stand for a few hours, or add a small pinch of salt to each litre (quart).

- When boiling water is not practical, you can treat water with chlorine tablets, iodine tablets, or unperfumed household chlorine bleach (5.25% sodium hypochlorite). If you use chlorine tablets or iodine tablets, follow the package directions. If you use household chlorine bleach, add one drop of bleach per litre (quart) of water, or three drops if the water is cloudy. Stir and let sit for 30 minutes before drinking. The water should have a slight chlorine smell.

- Use a bleach solution to rinse water containers before reusing them. Use water storage tanks and other types of containers with caution. For example, firetruck storage tanks and previously used cans or bottles may be contaminated with microbes or chemicals.

- Fuel spills and chemical releases are common during floods. If your water smells like fuel or has a chemical odor, do not use it. Contact your local health department to ask for a chemical analysis of your water. Do not rely on untested devices for decontaminating water.

- Until you are told by municipal authorities that your water supply is safe, or until your well water tests safe according to approved methods, use boiled, bottled, or treated water.

ALERT Treating water with chlorine tablets, iodine tablets, or liquid bleach will kill bacteria but not parasitic organisms.

Danger: Carbon Monoxide

Carbon monoxide (CO) is an odorless, colorless gas that can cause sudden illness and death if you breathe it. If you are too hot or too cold or you need to prepare food, don't put yourself and your family at risk: look to friends or a community shelter for help. If you must use an alternative source of fuel or electricity, be sure to use it only outside and away from open windows.

CO is in the combustion fumes produced by small gasoline engines, stoves, generators, lanterns, and gas ranges, and by burning coal, charcoal, or wood. When power outages occur during emergencies such as hurricanes or winter storms, it's tempting to try to use alternative sources of fuel or electricity for heating, cooling, or cooking. Be careful. CO from these sources can build up in your home, garage, or camper and kill the people and animals inside.

Common symptoms of carbon monoxide poisoning are headache, dizziness, weakness, nausea, vomiting, chest pain, and confusion. People who are asleep or who have been drinking alcohol can die from CO poisoning before ever having symptoms. If you think you or anyone around you may have CO poisoning, consult a health care professional right away.

- Never use a gas range or oven to heat a home.

- Never use a charcoal grill, hibachi, lantern, or portable camping stove inside a home, tent, or camper.

- Never run a generator, pressure washer, or any other gasoline-powered engine inside a basement, garage, or other enclosed structure, even if the doors and windows are open, unless the equipment has been professionally installed and vented. Before using such equipment, check to make sure vents and flues are free of debris, especially if winds are high, because flying debris can block them.

- Never run a motor vehicle, generator, pressure washer, or any gasoline-powered engine outside an open window or door where exhaust can vent into an enclosed area. Never leave the motor running in a vehicle parked in an enclosed or partially enclosed space, such as a garage.

Residents of Padre Island and Corpus Christi, Texas, stream northwest towards San Antonio amid the wind and rain ahead of Category 4 Hurricane Bret (1999). FEMA / Dave Gatley

Safe Evacuation

If local authorities ask you to leave your home, they have a good reason to make this request, and you should heed their advice immediately. Listen to your radio or television and follow the instructions of emergency officials.

- Wear long-sleeved shirts, long pants, and sturdy shoes so you can be protected as much as possible.

- Take your emergency kit and cellphone. Take small valuables and important papers, but travel light.

- Take your pets with you. They may not be permitted in public shelters, so follow your plan to go to a friend's home or pet-friendly hotel.

- If instructed to do so, shut off water, electricity, and gas before leaving. Keep in mind that if you turn off the gas, a qualified technician must turn it back on when you return home. In a disaster, this might take some time.

- Leave a note saying where you are going.

- Lock your home and don't forget your key.

- Go to the meeting place designated in your Family Emergency Plan.

- Use travel routes specified by local authorities. Don't use shortcuts. You cannot be sure which areas are dangerous or impassable.

- Get in touch with the out-of-area emergency contact person identified in your Family Emergency Plan to let him or her know what has happened, that you are okay, and how to contact you. Alert this person to any separated family members.

- Register at a registration and inquiry center so you can be contacted by your loved ones or notified when it is safe to return home. If you go to an evacuation center, sign in at the registration desk.

- Listen to emergency authorities for the most accurate information about what is happening in your area, and follow their instructions.

CHAPTER 9

AFTER THE STORM

What to Expect

After a severe hurricane, life may take some time to begin to return to normal. The safety of buildings and houses may be compromised, and storm-damaged trees could fall over or drop heavy branches. Rubble or debris may block building exits and roads, making it dangerous or difficult to get out or walk around. Power lines may be loose or down on the ground, perhaps in contact with standing water, and there may be long-lasting power outages. The water supply may be contaminated or limited in quantity, and extensive flooding may cause sewage services to break down.

Workplaces and schools may be closed, and there could be temporary restrictions on transportation and other services. Hospitals, clinics, and mental health services may be strained or overwhelmed for a time. High-demand goods and services, such as gasoline and water or repair services may be scarce and expensive.

After the Storm Has Passed

- Above all, try to stay calm.

- If possible, put on sturdy shoes and protective clothing to help prevent injury from debris, especially broken glass.

- Check yourself and others for injuries. Call for medical help for the injured. If you have first aid training, use it, taking care of life-threatening situations first. Even if you do not have training, ensure that nothing is blocking the injured person's airway, help him or her to rest as comfortably as possible, and provide reassurance while you await help.

- Check on your neighbors, especially those who are elderly, have disabilities, live alone, or have small children.

- Check for structural damage to the building you're in. If you suspect it is unsafe, leave and do not re-enter. If you are in a high-rise building, do not use the elevator, even if the power is on. It may fail at any moment.

- Do not turn on light switches or light matches until you are sure there aren't any gas leaks or spilled flammable liquids. Use a flashlight to check the utilities.

- Confine your pets to keep them safe.

- Use the battery-powered radio from your emergency kit to listen for information and instructions. Do not use the telephone except to report a life-threatening injury because the lines must be free for official use.

- Do not shut off utilities unless they are damaged or leaking (a gas leak smells like rotten eggs) or if there is a fire. If you turn the gas off, don't turn it on again. That must be done by a qualified technician.

A downed streetlight in Halifax, Nova Scotia, after Hurricane Juan (2003).
Richard Knowles.

- If tap water is available, fill a bathtub and other containers in case the supply gets cut off. If there is no running water, remember that you may have water available in a hot water tank, toilet tank, or ice cube trays. Do not flush toilets if you suspect that sewer lines are broken.

Returning Home

- If you and your family have had to evacuate during a hurricane, there may be a delay before you can safely return. Wait for permission from the emergency measures authorities before entering a storm-affected area.

- Stay away from damaged buildings or structures until they have been examined and certified as safe by a building inspector or other government authority. You may want to wait to return to buildings during daylight hours, when it is easier to avoid hazards, particularly if the electricity is off and you have no lights.

- Leave immediately if you hear shifting or unusual noises that signal that the structure may fall, or if you smell gas or suspect a leak. If you smell gas, notify emergency authorities and do not turn on the lights, light matches, smoke, or do anything that could cause a spark. Do not return to the house until you are told it is safe to do so.

- If the house has been closed up for several days, enter briefly to open doors and windows. Let the house air out for at least 30 minutes before you stay inside for any length of time.

TIP

Record the details of storm damage to your home – by photograph or video, if possible – and immediately register the damage with your insurance agent and your municipality.

Electrical Hazards

Do not enter a flooded building unless you are sure the power is disconnected. If you can turn off the main power from a dry location, do so, even if lack of power will delay cleanup. If you would have to stand in water to access the main power switch, call an electrician to turn it off.

If there has been a power outage, have an electrician check your house's electrical system before turning the power on again. Do not use flood-damaged appliances, electrical outlets, switch boxes or breaker panels until they have been checked and cleaned by a qualified technician. After a power outage:

- If the main electric switch was turned off, make sure appliances are unplugged to prevent damage from a power surge when the power is restored.

- Replace the furnace flue (if it has been removed) and turn off the fuel to the standby heating unit.

- Switch on the main electric supply.

- Give the electrical system a chance to stabilize before reconnecting appliances. Turn the heating system thermostats up first. In a couple of minutes, restart the refrigerator and freezer. Wait 10 to 15 minutes before reconnecting other appliances.

NEVER turn power on or off yourself while standing in water.

Chemical Hazards

During flood recovery, you may encounter chemical hazards.

- Floodwaters may have buried containers of dangerous solvents and other industrial chemicals or moved them from their normal storage places.

- If you find propane tanks, contact police or the fire department immediately. Propane tanks pose a significant danger of fire or explosion.

- Car batteries, even those in floodwater, may still contain an electrical charge. Wear insulated gloves and handle them with extreme caution. Avoid contact with any acid that may have spilled from a damaged car battery.

Biological Hazards

- A flooded building that has been closed up for more than a few days is likely contaminated with mold, which can cause serious illness. If you suspect that mold is present, wear a face mask and disposable gloves during preliminary assessment as well as cleanup.

- Floodwaters may contain fecal material from overflowing sewage systems and agricultural and industrial waste. If open cuts or sores have been exposed to floodwater, wash them thoroughly with soap and apply an antibiotic ointment to discourage infection.

- Practice basic hygiene faithfully. Wash your hands vigorously with soap and bottled water or water that has been boiled or disinfected. Wash them before preparing food or eating, after toilet use, after participating in clean-up activities, and after handling articles contaminated with floodwater or sewage. Use an alcohol-based hand sanitizer if clean water is in short supply.

- Restore your home to good order as soon as possible to protect your health and prevent further damage to the house and its contents. Flood-damaged household items must be discarded according to local regulations, and all surfaces must be disinfected.

- Keep children and pets out of the affected area until the cleanup has been completed.

Keep Food Safe

Having survived the storm, you need to protect your own and your family's health by eating only uncontaminated food that is not decayed. Identify and throw away food that may not be safe to eat, prepare and store food safely, and keep infants safe from deadly contaminated food or water.

Sorting Good from Bad

- Throw away food that may have come in contact with flood or storm water.

- Throw away food that has an unusual odor, color, or texture.

- Throw away perishable foods (including meat, poultry, fish, eggs, and leftovers) that have been above 4°C (40°F) for 2 hours or more.

- Thawed food that contains ice crystals or is 4°C (40°F) or cooler can be refrozen or cooked.

- Throw away canned foods if the cans are bulging, opened, or damaged.

- Food in containers with screw caps, snap lids, crimped caps (such as beer bottles), twist caps, and fliptops, and home canned foods should be discarded if they have come into contact with floodwater because they cannot be disinfected.

A child carrying ice home in the U.S. Virgin Islands after Hurricane Marilyn (1995). FEMA

- If cans have come in contact with floodwater or storm water, remove the labels, wash the cans, and dip them in a solution of 250 ml (1 cup) of bleach to 19 litres (5 gallons) of water. Relabel the cans with a marker.

Storage and Preparation

- While the power is out, keep the refrigerator and freezer doors closed as much as possible.

- Add block ice or dry ice to your refrigerator if the electricity is expected to be off longer than 4 hours. Wear heavy gloves when handling ice.

- Do not use contaminated water to wash dishes, brush your teeth, wash and prepare food, wash your hands, make ice, or make baby formula.

- Clean and sanitize surfaces that come in contact with food. Discard wooden cutting boards, baby bottle nipples, and pacifiers, which cannot be properly sanitized. Clean and sanitize other food-contact surfaces in a four-step process:

    - Wash with soap and clean warm water.

    - Rinse with clean water.

    - Sanitize by immersing for one minute in a solution made by mixing 5 ml (1 teaspoon) of unperfumed household chlorine bleach with 4 litres (1 gallon) of clean water.

    - Allow to air dry.

Feeding Infants
Breastfed infants should continue breastfeeding. For formula-fed infants, use ready-to-feed formula if possible. If this is unavailable, use bottled water to prepare powdered or concentrated formula. If bottled water is not available, use boiled water. Use treated water to prepare formula only if you do not have bottled or boiled water.

- If you prepare formula with boiled water, be sure it is cool before giving it to an infant.

- Clean feeding bottles and nipples with bottled, boiled, or treated water before each use.

- Wash your hands before preparing formula and before feeding an infant. You can use alcohol-based hand sanitizer for washing your hands if the water supply is limited

Keep Water Safe

Water may not be safe to drink, clean with, or bathe in after an emergency such as a hurricane or flood. During and after a disaster, it may be contaminated with micro-organisms such as bacteria, sewage, agricultural or industrial waste, chemicals, and other substances that can cause illness or death.

Listen to and follow public announcements. Local authorities will tell you if tap water is safe to drink or to use for cooking or bathing. If the water is not safe to use, follow local instructions to use bottled water or to boil or disinfect water for cooking, cleaning, or bathing.

Use only bottled, boiled, or treated water for drinking, cooking or preparing food, washing dishes, cleaning, brushing your teeth, washing your hands, making ice, and bathing until your water supply is tested and found safe. If your water supply is limited, you can use alcohol-based hand sanitizer for washing your hands.

Be cautious when using water from storage tanks or storing water in other containers. Storage tanks and previously used cans or jugs may be contaminated with microbes or chemicals. Before use, water containers should be thoroughly cleaned, then rinsed with a bleach solution.

Private wells must be tested and disinfected after flood waters recede. If your well may be contaminated, contact your local health department for specific advice.

CHAPTER 10

CLEANUP AND RECOVERY

Cleaning up your home after the extensive water damage caused by a hurricane is a huge and disheartening task. Assessing what is dangerous and what is just hard, dirty work and breaking the job into steps will help you tackle it with confidence.

Recommended Equipment

- Strong rubber gloves

- Sturdy work gloves

- Masks, goggles, earplugs, and other protective gear

- Pails, mops, squeegees, and rags

- Wet-dry shop vacuum cleaner

- Plastic garbage bags

- Unscented non-ammonia detergent

- Household chlorine bleach

82nd Airborne troops and local law enforcement officials trying to move a house from the middle of a flooded road in Vermilion Parish, Louisiana, after Hurricane Rita (2005). U.S. Army / PFC Jacqueline M. Haw

- Large containers for soaking bedding, clothing and linens, and clothes lines to hang them to dry

First Steps

Water Damage

- Do not occupy a house that still contains standing water.

- Do not heat your home to more than 4°C (40°F) until all of the water is removed.

- Immediately add about 2 litres (2 quarts) of chlorine bleach to standing water.

- If the water in your home is deep, remove it in stages — about a third of the volume daily. If the ground is still saturated and you pump out your house too quickly, the outside water pressure can make the walls or the floor buckle.

- Use pumps or pails first to remove standing water, and then use a wet-dry shop vacuum to suck up the rest.

- For instructions on how to disinfect and restore wells and cisterns, contact your local health authorities or emergency measures organization.

If you use gasoline, kerosene, or propane powered pumps or heaters, buy and install a carbon monoxide sensor. Carbon monoxide in exhaust fumes can kill you if it builds up in your work area.

Dirt and Debris

- Remove all soaked and dirty materials as well as debris.

- Remove furniture, appliances, clothing, bedding, and residual mud.

- Hose off any dirt sticking to walls and solid wood furniture. Rinse several times.

- Wash and wipe down all surfaces and structures with chlorine bleach, ensuring there is adequate cross-ventilation to remove fumes. Then rinse again.

- Wipe down all interior walls, floors, and other surfaces that have not been directly affected by the flood using a solution of one part chlorine bleach to four parts cold or tepid water, mixed with a small amount of non-ammonia detergent. Then rinse and dry thoroughly.

- Carpets must be dried within the first two days. For large areas, hire a qualified professional to do the job. Carpets soaked with sewage must be discarded immediately.

ALERT

Wear a charcoal respirator when using bleach in any closed space.

Buildings

- Rinse, then clean all floors as quickly as possible to give yourself a reasonably clean work area.

- Break out walls and remove and discard drywall, wood paneling and insulation at least 50 centimetres (20 inches) above the high-water line.

- Remove and discard flooring that has been deeply penetrated by floodwater or sewage.

- Thoroughly clean all remaining hard surfaces such as flooring, concrete, molding, wood and metal furniture, countertops, appliances, sinks, and other plumbing fixtures with hot water and laundry or dish detergent.

- Ventilate or dehumidify the building until it is completely dry. Tape clear food wrap to sections of material. If these sections are still damp inside, they will turn darker than the surrounding material. Dry until this does not occur.

- Check flooded areas regularly. If you find mold, kill it immediately by washing with chlorine bleach. Mold can lead to serious health problems.

Cleanup Safety Tips

General

- Have at least two fire extinguishers at every clean-up job.

- Keep children away from contaminated areas.

- Wear a hard hat, goggles, heavy work gloves, and watertight boots with steel toe and insole (not just steel shank) for structural cleanup.

- Wear earplugs or protective headphones to reduce risk from equipment noise.

- Use teams of two or more people to move bulky objects.

- Operate chainsaws according to manufacturer's instructions, wear appropriate protective equipment, avoid contact with power lines, and be sure that bystanders are at a safe distance. Take extra care when cutting trees or branches that are bent or caught under another object, in case they spring back. When using an electric chainsaw, use extreme caution to avoid electrical shock.

- If there has been a backflow of sewage, wear rubber boots, rubber gloves, and goggles while cleaning up the affected area.

- Wear a charcoal respirator mask when using bleach in any closed space.

- In hot weather, try to stay cool by taking breaks in shaded areas or in cool rooms, drinking water and non-alcoholic fluids often, and wearing lightweight and loose-fitting clothing. Work outdoors during cooler hours.

- Continue to monitor your radio or television for up-to-date emergency information.

Never turn power on or off or use an electric tool or appliance while standing in water. You could be electrocuted.

Electricity

- If electrical circuits and electrical equipment have gotten wet or are in or near water, turn off the power at the main breaker or fuse on the service panel. Do this only if you can stand somewhere dry. Otherwise, call an electrician.

- Do not connect generators to your home's electrical circuits without approved automatic-interrupt devices. If a generator is on line when electrical service is restored, it can become a major fire hazard, and it may endanger line workers helping to restore power in your area.

Hazardous Materials

- Call the fire department to inspect or remove chemicals, propane and other fuel tanks, and other dangerous materials.

- Wear protective clothing and gear, such as a respirator, when handling hazardous materials.

- Wash skin that may have come in contact with hazardous materials.

- Wear insulated gloves and use caution if you have to remove a car battery. Avoid any acid that may have leaked from it.

Hygiene and Infectious Disease Prevention

- In breaks from cleaning up and when you're finished for the day, wash thoroughly with soap and water. If there is a boil-water advisory in effect, use water that has been boiled for 1 minute and cooled. Or you may use water that has been chemically disinfected for personal hygiene.

- The water in a flooded building may contain fecal material from overflowing sewage systems and agricultural and industrial waste. Although skin contact with floodwater does not, by itself, pose a serious health risk, there is risk of disease from eating or drinking anything contaminated with floodwater and from contaminating your own food and drink with unwashed hands.

- If open cuts or sores have been exposed to floodwater, wash them well with soap and water and apply an antibiotic ointment to discourage infection.

- Wash all clothes worn during the cleanup in hot water and detergent. These clothes should be washed separately from uncontaminated clothes and household linens.

- To reduce cold–related risks when standing or working in water which is cooler than 24°C (75°F), wear insulated clothes and insulated rubber boots, take frequent breaks out of the water, and change into dry clothing whenever possible.

- Seek immediate medical attention if you are injured or become ill.

Keep or Discard?

- Remove and discard all insulation materials.

- Discard all soaked items that cannot be washed and disinfected, including carpet and carpet underlay, rugs, mattresses and box springs, pillows, stuffed toys and baby toys, foam-rubber items, books, wall coverings, cosmetics and other personal care products, paper products, particleboard furniture, upholstered furniture, and furniture coverings, padding, and cushions.

- Frames of high-quality furniture can often be saved. However, they must first be cleaned, disinfected, and rinsed, then dried by ventilation away from direct sunlight or heat. Drying too quickly can cause warping and cracking.

- Scrape heavy dirt from washable clothes. Wash and rinse them several times with detergent and dry them quickly.

- Consult your lawyer to determine whether flood-damaged documents, or just the information in them, must be retained.

- Clear the yard of all debris and refuse. It can provide a breeding ground for bacteria and mold, and it can harbor vermin such as rats.

Flood-Damaged Treasures

- Sewage-contaminated household items must be bagged, tagged, and discarded according to local health regulations.

- You may be able to save items that are simply water-damaged. Act quickly to prevent further damage, and move items to a cool, dry place.

- Books, documents, and textiles can be placed in a freezer until they can be properly treated.

- Wet items will be heavy and fragile, so keep them well supported when handling, drying, or freezing.

TIP

Consult a professional conservator before attempting repairs of antiques and heirlooms.

Salvaging What You Can

- Most things can be air-dried. Move items to a cool, dry place and set up fans. If you do this outdoors, keep them out of direct sunlight.

- Dirty items that are saturated can be rinsed with clean water if they are strong enough to withstand it. Exceptions are paper, fragile items, and items with loose parts or soluble paints and adhesives. If items are just damp, let mud dry and then brush it off.

- Mold is a health hazard; if mold is present, wear a face mask and disposable gloves. To minimize mold growth, move items to a cool, dry area within 48 hours and set up fans. Wet mold will smear if wiped; let it dry and then brush it off outdoors. Materials that would not be harmed by alcohol can be lightly misted with isopropanol (rubbing alcohol) to kill mold spores.

- Freezing can temporarily halt further damage. Freezing is appropriate for books, paper documents, furs, and textiles. Gently blot (do not wring) furs and textiles first with toweling to remove excess water, and keep them well supported. Place items in individual plastic bags or separate with wax paper to keep them from sticking together when frozen.

Dry Out Your Home

- If you have electricity, and an electrician has determined that it's safe to turn it on, use a wet-dry shop vacuum, or the vacuum function of a carpet steam cleaner, an electric-powered water transfer pump, or a sump pump to remove standing water. If you are operating equipment in wet areas, be sure to wear rubber boots to keep from electrocuting yourself.

- If weather permits, open windows and doors to aid in the drying-out process.

- Use fans and dehumidifiers to remove excess moisture. Fans should be placed at a window or door to blow the air outwards, rather than inwards, to avoid spreading mold.

- If your home heating, ventilating, and air-conditioning (HVAC) system was flooded, it will be contaminated with mold, and turning it on will spread mold throughout the house. Have the system checked and cleaned by a maintenance or service professional who is experienced in mold cleanup before you turn it on. Professional cleaning will kill the mold and prevent later mold growth. Once the system is clean, and when turning it on is safe otherwise, you can use it to help remove moisture from your home.

- Ensure that crawl spaces in basements have proper drainage to limit water seepage. Ventilate to allow the area to dry out.

- Prevent water outdoors from re-entering your home. Rainwater from gutters or the roof should drain away from the house. The ground around the house should slope away from it to keep basements and crawl spaces dry.

U.S. Army Major Timothy A. Doherty, 148th Medical Co. Georgia Army National Guard, searches for stranded New Orleans citizens on September 4, 2005, after Hurricane Katrina ravaged the city.
U.S. Army / Department of Defense

Before Moving Back In

Even though the floodwaters may have receded and you can get back to your home, you must not live there until:

- the regular water supply has been inspected and officially declared safe for use;

- every flood-contaminated room has been thoroughly cleaned, disinfected, and surface-dried;

- all contaminated dishes and utensils have been thoroughly washed and disinfected. Either boil them or wash them in a sterilizing solution of one part chlorine bleach to four parts water and rinse thoroughly; and

- adequate toilet facilities are available.

Listen for and follow directions from your local health authority.

Heating Systems and Appliances

- Do not use flooded appliances, electrical outlets, switch boxes, or breaker panels until they have been checked by your local utility.

- Whether you use a wood, gas, or electrical heating system, ensure that it has been thoroughly inspected by a qualified technician before using it again.

- Replace the furnace blower motor, switches, and controls if they have been soaked. Flooded forced-air heating ducts and return-duct pans should be either cleaned or replaced.

- Replace filters and insulation inside furnaces, water heaters, refrigerators, and freezers if they have been wet. Replacing the appliance may be less expensive.

Drains

- Flush and disinfect floor drains and sump pumps with detergent and water. Scrub them to remove greasy dirt and grime.

- Clean or replace clogged footing drains outside the foundation. Consult a professional for advice or service.

The Road to Recovery

People caught in a major disaster often feel confused. Immediately afterwards, they are likely to feel relieved to be alive but bewildered and shocked.

At first, you may tremble, feel numb, vomit, or faint, and later you might not act like yourself for a while. You may feel apathetic or angry. Many survivors sleep poorly, have no appetite, are angry with those around them, or panic at the slightest hint of danger. These feelings and reactions are perfectly normal.

Talk about your feelings. Discuss what's happened. Recognize that grieving is a natural reaction to suffering a loss. While you are doing your best to clean up the mess and recover what you can, give yourself and those around you permission to grieve and time to heal.

A teddy bear in the aftermath of Hurricane Katrina (2005). U.S. Marine Corps / Lance Cpl. Daniel J. Klein

Helping Children

Children exposed to a disaster can experience a range of responses such as anxiety, fear, nervousness, stomach aches, loss of appetite, and sleep problems. They might resume thumb-sucking or bedwetting or suffer from bad dreams. These are normal and temporary reactions to danger. Parents can help relieve their children's anxiety by taking their fears seriously, reassuring them, and giving them additional attention and affection.

After a disaster, children are most afraid that the event will happen again, that someone will get hurt or injured, that they will be separated from the family, or that they will be left alone. Comfort and reassure them. Tell them what you know about the situation. Be honest but gentle. Encourage them to talk about the disaster and ask questions. Give

132

them a real task to do, something that helps get the family back on its feet. Do not expose them to clean-up hazards, which can be significant, but keep them with you even if it seems easier to do things on your own. At a time like this, it's important for the whole family to stay together.

CHECKLISTS

First Aid Kit

- ❑ First aid manual
- ❑ Adhesive bandages in several sizes
- ❑ Gauze pads
- ❑ Elastic bandage
- ❑ Adhesive tape
- ❑ Cotton swabs
- ❑ Safety pins
- ❑ Scissors
- ❑ Thermometer
- ❑ Tweezers
- ❑ Instant disposable cold pack
- ❑ Cleansing agent (e.g. hydrogen peroxide) or soap
- ❑ Antibiotic ointment
- ❑ Antiseptic wipes
- ❑ Calamine lotion
- ❑ Hydrocortisone cream
- ❑ Eyewash solution
- ❑ Over-the-counter pain relievers (e.g. acetaminophen, ibuprofen)
- ❑ CPR mouth shield
- ❑ Disposable gloves (2 pairs)

Emergency Kit

- ❏ Flashlight
- ❏ Battery or crank radio
- ❏ Batteries (stored separately in a waterproof bag)
- ❏ First aid kit
- ❏ Candles and matches or lighter
- ❏ Extra car and house keys.
- ❏ Extra cash, including coins or telephone cards
- ❏ Important papers, including identification for everyone likely to be in your party and personal documents
- ❏ Food and bottled water
- ❏ Clothing and footwear (one change per person)
- ❏ Blankets or sleeping bags (one blanket or sleeping bag per person)
- ❏ Toilet paper
- ❏ Sanitary pads and other personal supplies
- ❏ Medication
- ❏ Whistle (to attract help)
- ❏ Backpack, duffel bag, or other container in which to carry the emergency kit if evacuation is necessary

Additional Household Emergency Items

- ❏ Gasoline-powered generator and appropriately rated extension cord
- ❏ Camp stove and fuel
- ❏ Portable toilet
- ❏ Books, playing cards, games, toys, coloring books, paper, crayons
- ❏ Small up-to-date photos of family and loved ones for identification
- ❏ Moist towelettes
- ❏ Facial tissues
- ❏ Comb or hairbrush, shampoo, deodorant
- ❏ Liquid detergent
- ❏ Insect repellent
- ❏ Plastic garbage bags and ties
- ❏ Chlorine bleach, liquid disinfectant

Vehicle Emergency Kit

- ❑ Booster cables, tools, tow chains
- ❑ Shovel and sand, kitty litter, or other traction aid
- ❑ Ice scraper and brush
- ❑ Warning lights or road flares, axe or hatchet, fire extinguisher, seatbelt cutter
- ❑ Extra windshield washer fluid, fuel-line de-icer, antifreeze
- ❑ Map of your region
- ❑ Bottled water, at least 4 litres (1 gallon)
- ❑ Canned food and opener, dried fruit, cookies, crackers
- ❑ Outdoor clothing, footwear, backpack
- ❑ Sleeping bag(s) or emergency thermal blankets
- ❑ First aid kit and manual
- ❑ Compass
- ❑ Flashlight, batteries (store separately in waterproof bags)
- ❑ Waterproof matches
- ❑ An unscented plain candle in a deep can, to warm hands, heat a drink, or use as an emergency light
- ❑ Roll of paper towel, toilet paper, moist towelettes, small plastic bags
- ❑ Cash, coins for using a public telephone
- ❑ Pen, pencil, paper
- ❑ Playing cards, coloring books, crayons for children
- ❑ Cellphone

Workplace Emergency Kit

- ❑ Gloves, walking shoes, outdoor clothing
- ❑ Emergency silver foil ("space") blanket
- ❑ Flashlight
- ❑ Radio
- ❑ Batteries (stored separately in a waterproof bag)
- ❑ Whistle
- ❑ Bottled water
- ❑ Dried fruit and nuts, high-energy food bars
- ❑ Small up-to-date photos of family and loved ones for identification
- ❑ Personal identification, including your name, home address, next-of-kin contact information, and emergency medical information

Important Documents

- ❑ Will
- ❑ Power of attorney
- ❑ Insurance policies and life insurance beneficiary designations
- ❑ Contracts
- ❑ Deeds
- ❑ Stocks and bonds
- ❑ Family records, such as birth and marriage certificates
- ❑ Passport
- ❑ Social Insurance or Social Security card
- ❑ Health care and medical insurance cards, immunization records
- ❑ Licenses
- ❑ Savings and checking account numbers
- ❑ Credit card account numbers, company contact information
- ❑ Important telephone numbers
- ❑ Printed copies of emergency checklists and instructions

GLOSSARY

Cape Verde-type hurricanes: Atlantic basin tropical cyclones that develop into tropical storms less than1,000 kilometres (620 miles) from the Cape Verde Islands, off the west coast of Africa, and become hurricanes before reaching the Caribbean Sea. Typically, these occur in August and September.

Coriolis Force: Apparent effect of the earth's rotation that tends to turn the direction of any object or fluid clockwise (toward the right) in the northern hemisphere and counterclockwise (toward the left) in the southern hemisphere. The Coriolis Force gives a tropical cyclone its spin.

Cumulus Clouds: Heaped or lumpy clouds that form when conditions in the atmosphere are unstable.

Cumulonimbus Clouds: Clouds that are exceptionally dense and vertically developed, looking like mountains or towers. The tops, which are at the top of the troposphere, spread out like a blacksmith's anvil. Commonly recognized as thunderclouds.

Cyclone: An area of low pressure around which winds blow counterclockwise in the Northern Hemisphere. **Cyclone** is also the term used for a hurricane in the western Pacific and Indian oceans.

El Niño: A warming of Pacific Ocean waters near the Equator that typically occurs every three to seven years and creates a shift in normal weather patterns. La Niña, conversely, is a cooling of the equatorial Pacific waters.

Eye: The area of calm at the heart of a storm, where the sky may be clear and there is little or no wind.

Eye wall: The ring of thunderstorms surrounding a storm's eye, where the heaviest rain, strongest winds, and worst turbulence normally occur.

Hurricane: A cyclone of tropical origin with wind speeds of at least 118 kilometres (74 miles or 64 knots) per hour.

Hurricane Track: The line along which the eye of a hurricane moves.

Hurricane Season: The months of the year when hurricanes are most common. The hurricane season in the Atlantic, Caribbean, and Gulf of Mexico runs from June 1 to November 30.

Knot: A measurement of speed at sea. 1 knot = 1 nautical mile per hour. This is equivalent to approximately 1.2 (statute) miles or 1.9 kilometres per hour. One nautical mile = 1 minute of latitude at the equator.

Landfall: Where a hurricane touches the coastline. The hurricane eye landfall is the spot at which the eye, or physical center, of the hurricane reaches the coastline.

Low Pressure System: An area with a central air pressure lower than the air pressure of its surroundings. Storm systems are all low pressure systems.

Millibar: A metric measurement of air pressure. 1 inch of mercury = 33.87 millibars.

Post-Tropical Storm: A tropical storm or hurricane that moves beyond the tropics into the mid-latitudes and begins losing its tropical characteristics.

Saffir-Simpson Scale: A numerical system of classifying hurricanes that enables public safety officials to assess potential wind and storm surge damage. Category 1 is the least dangerous; Category 5 is the most dangerous.

Spiral Rain Bands: Bands of thunderstorms that wrap around the eye of a hurricane.

Storm Surge: The high, forceful dome of wind-driven water that sweeps along the coastline near where the eye passes close to the coast or makes landfall.

Trade Winds: Surface winds in the low-level air flow within the tropical easterlies.

Tropical Cyclone: The generic term for a class of tropical weather systems that includes tropical depressions, tropical storms, and hurricanes.

Tropical Depression: A tropical cyclone with maximum sustained surface winds less than 63 kilometres (39 miles or 34 knots) per hour.

Tropical Storm: A tropical cyclone with maximum sustained surface winds between 63 and 117 kilometres (39-73 miles or 34-63 knots) per hour.

Troposphere: Lowermost layer of the atmosphere, in which air temperature falls steadily with increasing altitude. All weather occurs in the troposphere.

Trough: An elongated area of low barometric pressure.

Typhoon: A hurricane in the northern Pacific Ocean west of the International Date Line.

Updraft: A small-scale current of air moving vertically upward. The moisture in it may condense, forming a cumulus cloud and possibly thunderstorms. A downdraft is a downward-moving air current.

Vertical Wind Shear: The magnitude of wind change with height. Vertical wind shear can weaken or destroy a hurricane by interfering with the organization of deep convection around its center.

RESOURCES

Weather Information and Climatology

Canadian Hurricane Centre (CHC)
www.atl.ec.gc.ca/weather/hurricane
45 Alderney Drive, Dartmouth, Nova Scotia, Canada B2Y 2N6

Environment Canada
www.ec.gc.ca
Inquiry Centre, 70 Crémazie Street, Gatineau, Quebec, Canada
K1A 0H3

Hurricane Hunters
www.hurricanehunters.com

Meteorological Service of Canada (MSC)
www.msc-smc.ec.gc.ca

National Hurricane Center (NHC)
www.nhc.noaa.gov
Tropical Prediction Center, 11691 S.W. 17th Street, Miami, Florida,
U.S.A. 33165-2149

National Oceanic and Atmospheric Administration (NOAA)
www.noaa.gov
NOAA Public Affairs, U.S. Department of Commerce, 14th Street
and Constitution Avenue NW, Room 6217, Washington, D.C.,
U.S.A. 20230

National Weather Service (NWS)
www.nws.noaa.gov
1325 East West Highway, Silver Spring, Maryland, U.S.A.
20910

Emergency Preparedness

Canadians can find out about the most common risks in each region by consulting the Canadian Disaster Database (ocipep. gc.ca/disaster) and the Natural Hazards of Canada map, available on the Internet at atlas.gc.ca/site/english/maps/environment/ naturalhazards or through Public Safety and Emergency Preparedness Canada (PSEPC).

Information about disaster risks the United States can be obtained from local American Red Cross chapters, state and local emergency measures offices, the Federal Emergency Management Agency (FEMA), or on the Internet at Hazardmaps. gov.

American Red Cross
www.redcross.org
National Headquarters, 2025 E Street N.W., Washington, DC, U.S.A 20006

Canadian Red Cross
www.redcross.ca
National Office, 170 Metcalfe Street, Suite 300, Ottawa, Ontario, Canada K2P 2P2

Centers for Disease Control and Prevention
www.bt.cdc.gov/disasters/hurricanes
1600 Clifton Road, Atlanta, Georgia, U.S.A 30333

Federal Emergency Management Agency (FEMA)
www.fema.gov
500 C Street S.W., Washington, D.C., U.S.A 20472

Public Safety and Emergency Preparedness Canada (PSEPC)
www.psepc-sppcc.gc.ca
340 Laurier Avenue West, Ottawa, Ontario, Canada K1A 0P8

INDEX TO HURRICANES

ACKNOWLEDGEMENTS

The information in this book comes from many sources, all of them freely available to everyone. These include: Environment Canada Meteorological Service of Canada, Canadian Hurricane Centre (CHC); Halifax Regional Municipality; Public Safety and Emergency Preparedness Canada (PSEPC); Toronto and Region Conservation Authority (TRCA); U.S. Air Force and Air Force Reserve; U.S. Army; U.S. Department of Defence; U.S. Environmental Protection Agency (EPA); U.S. Department of Health and Human Services Centers for Disease Control and Prevention (CDC); U.S. Department of Homeland Security; U.S. Federal Emergency Management Agency (FEMA); National Aeronautics and Space Administration (NASA); U.S. Dept. of Commerce National Oceanic and Atmospheric Administration (NOAA), National Climatic Data Center (NCDC), National Data Buoy Center, National Hurricane Center (NHC), National Weather Service (NWS); U.S. Marine Corps; U.S. Navy. Every effort has been made to secure permission to reproduce copyrighted materials. If any copyright holder has not been reached, please contact Goose Lane Editions at gooselane@gooselane.com.

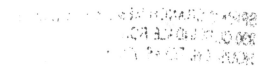